Teaching Notes on Piano Exam Pieces 2007–2008

Grades 1–7

TIMOTHY BARRATT
JULIAN HELLABY
VANESSA LATARCHE
MARGARET MURRAY McLEOD
ANTHONY WILLIAMS

Teaching Notes on Piano Exam Pieces 2007–2008

Grades 1–7

With an introduction by CLARA TAYLOR, Chief Examiner of The Associated Board of the Royal Schools of Music

The Associated Board of the Royal Schools of Music

First published in 2006 by
The Associated Board of the Royal Schools of Music (Publishing) Limited
24 Portland Place, London W1B 1LU, United Kingdom

ISBN 10: 1 86096 677 2
ISBN 13: 978 1 86096 677 4

AB 3205

A CIP catalogue for this book is available from The British Library.

Typeset by Hope Services (Abingdon) Ltd
Printed in England by Caligraving Limited, Thetford, Norfolk

CONTENTS

NOTES ON CONTRIBUTORS

Timothy Barratt, ARAM GRSM LRAM ARCM LMusTCL, is a professor at the Royal Academy of Music and Head of Keyboard at Dulwich College, London. He has toured extensively and broadcast as a solo pianist, accompanist and chamber music player. He adjudicates, directs workshops for teachers and is an Associated Board examiner, trainer and moderator, and a mentor for the Board's Certificate of Teaching.

Julian Hellaby, MMus LRAM ARAM, studied piano at the Royal Academy of Music and has performed throughout the UK and overseas. He is an Associated Board examiner, trainer and moderator, and a mentor for the Board's Certificate of Teaching course. He has extensive experience of piano teaching at all levels, and is currently Associate Senior Lecturer at Coventry University. His CD recordings include four of contemporary British piano music, of which one is piano duos (with pianist Peter Noke).

Vanessa Latarche, Hon ARAM FTCL LRAM ARCM, has established a reputation as a leading teacher. She is Head of Keyboard at the Royal College of Music, London and an Associated Board moderator, trainer, examiner and presenter, working internationally in most capacities. As a performer she enjoys a busy concert schedule and gives broadcasts for the BBC. She is also an experienced adjudicator and gives masterclasses in the UK and abroad.

Margaret Murray McLeod, ARAM FTCL LRAM ARCM, studied piano and composition at the Royal Academy of Music. As well as performing as a soloist and accompanist, she has many years' experience of teaching at all levels. From 1972 she trained student teachers and performers at Napier University, Edinburgh, where she was Senior Lecturer for Performance Studies until 1997. Her work as a lecturer, examiner and adjudicator has taken her worldwide.

Anthony Williams, MMus Dip.RAM GRSM LRAM, has an active performing, teaching and adjudicating career in the UK and abroad and is currently Head of Keyboard and Instrumental Music at Radley College, Oxfordshire. He is an examiner (jazz and classical), trainer and moderator for the Associated Board as well as a mentor for its Certificate of Teaching. He is the co-author of previous *Teaching Notes*, with Clara Taylor, and the compiler of *Fingerprints* (Faber, 2002), a collection of original repertoire for piano teaching.

INTRODUCTION

Teachers always enjoy sharing professional insights. The contributors to these *Teaching Notes* – all distinguished teachers as well as being examiners – are no exception. Their enthusiasm shines out of the text and I know they have relished the detailed investigation into this exciting new syllabus. Writing commentaries is, of course, a very time-consuming exercise and regretfully it is no longer possible for me to be a regular contributor with the ever-increasing demands of the Associated Board's new initiatives. However, I am retaining a close interest and connection with these notes and take pleasure in providing the introduction.

The wide choice of repertoire for every grade gives the opportunity to match the pieces to the pupil. Sometimes you might choose a style that immediately suits, and at other times you might take a more medicinal approach in order to tackle shortcomings. From the lists there are obvious winners, which will appear many times in the exams, but do also explore the alternative pieces not published in the graded volumes. There are some delights to be found that may just be the answer for some pupils.

From Grade 1 to Grade 8 the three lists have more in common than you might expect. List A contains the technically demanding repertoire, List B the more warmly expressive pieces, and List C has a tremendous variety of styles, often with some jazzy rhythms. Despite the enormous difference in standards between Grade 1 and Grade 8, candidates' strengths and weaknesses tend to follow predictable paths in each list. I believe it will be helpful, therefore, to consider the three lists in more detail.

LIST A

In List A, definition of fingerwork, clarity of articulation and control of co-ordination are necessary, as fluency increases through the grades. These technical challenges, especially runs and ornaments, can upset the basic rhythm, and in their determination some candidates use an over-emphatic heavy touch that is self-defeating. An ability to keep the hands in exact ensemble is needed. Examiners often hear hands starting together then parting company at difficult corners. In higher grades, part-playing will often be a feature in List A and it's fairly rare to hear this successfully achieved. Many candidates over-emphasize the subject without adjusting the balance of the other lines. When this happens, control of dynamics and phrasing is inevitably affected.

Ornaments can be simplified or omitted in the early grades if they are causing problems with the rhythm. A steady basic beat is, of course, a higher priority than the decorations. In later grades some ornamentation is often necessary and certainly needs to be included to achieve higher marks.

In their efforts to manage the technicalities, many candidates are less aware of the musical content of the List A pieces. It's a delight to hear the right texture, clear dynamics and musical phrasing capturing the elegant style of the repertoire, which often comes from quite an early era.

LIST B

List B gives every opportunity to show more expressive phrasing and tonal warmth. The pieces are selected mostly from the Classical or Romantic styles, and cantabile tone will be needed for the melodies. Phrasing comes right to the forefront and balance of hands needs real care, as these pieces often follow the pattern of right-hand melody and left-hand accompaniment. Pedalling will be necessary for the more legato choices, with clean, rhythmic legato pedalling requiring good physical co-ordination. Even in higher grades we frequently hear the hands and the right foot not really coinciding.

Rubato is a vital part of musical phrasing and is often needed in the List B pieces. Candidates are usually better at slowing up than getting faster, so it will be helpful to explain the concept of a balanced rubato during the practice period.

Dynamics tend to be more smoothly graded in the styles chosen for this list, and ability to mould the tone evenly in each hand is something to aim for at all stages. Subtlety of tone colour and control of rubato within the stylistic discipline of the pieces are high priorities. Often the pieces have descriptive titles, giving a clue to the mood and atmosphere of the music.

LIST C

This list offers something for everyone. These days there is tremendous variety – jazz pieces, contemporary items and a host of other styles – which should make it easy to find exactly the right choice for your pupils.

In the early grades the jazz items are always hugely popular. Candidates can manage quite difficult rhythms when they like the music. Strongly rhythmic, dynamic pieces, such as the all-time hit *The Swinging Sioux* from the 1999–2000 Grade 1 syllabus, seem to capture the imagination of thousands of candidates throughout the world.

With such variety on offer, it's important to go to the heart of what each piece really requires to make an effective performance. Very often this means having a feel for the underlying beat, which will be more pronounced in the jazz pieces but still vital in many contemporary items. Colourful playing, evoking the various moods and sound worlds, will be enjoyable to explore, and candidates often feel they can relax and communicate these pieces, achieving more of a sense of performance than they manage with pieces from either of the two other lists.

Swung rhythm is an issue right from Grade 1. This is not the place to give a detailed description (which really needs a demonstration to make the point), but pupils will be helped imagining that 4/4 time becomes 12/8, so that a dotted-quaver, semiquaver rhythm sounds more like crotchet, quaver. Pupils often catch on to this in certain parts of the piece, but find it difficult to be consistent, therefore causing the examiner to comment: 'Try to keep an even rhythm.' This does not mean that the swung rhythm has not been noticed, but usually indicates that there's an inconsistency in managing this throughout the performance. It is also perfectly acceptable to play the piece 'straight', especially in the lower grades, as long as the mood and relaxed feel of this style still come across. In the higher grades, the jazz pieces are quite sophisticated and often need a sense of swing and appreciation of whichever jazz style is appropriate to the piece.

In List C the metronome mark is often the composer's, so it pays to take notice and check carefully; as in Lists A and B, a metronome mark in square brackets indicates that it is an editorial suggestion, allowing a little more freedom of choice.

Young pupils often have a refreshingly open mind about contemporary items. Teachers may find some of the pieces slightly off-putting, but may be surprised to find that their students can get inside the music quite quickly and thoroughly enjoy playing in a different idiom.

Candidates are free to choose the order of their three pieces. It may well be wise to put the more technically demanding List A piece somewhere other than first in the exam. Many pupils these days start with their favourite piece, which helps confidence when they come to tackle the others. It is sometimes rather disappointingly obvious why a piece has been left until last!

The extensive selection for each grade should ensure that each one of your candidates is happy and comfortable with the choice and order of his or her pieces. As teachers will be well aware, the candidate's attitude of mind as he or she comes into the exam room is inevitably reflected in the result.

If you have any queries arising from this publication, do not hesitate to contact me, preferably by email (chiefexaminer@abrsm.ac.uk).

All good wishes to users of these notes, who will be inspired and reassured as the excellent selection of pieces becomes the graded pianistic diet for the coming exam sessions.

Clara Taylor

GRADE 1

Pupils will usually have been learning for up to eighteen months by the time Grade 1 is on the horizon. They may have taken the Prep Test during this time, in which case they will probably feel quite confident when facing this first real exam. A wide choice of pieces should help to keep motivation high, so why not have some alternatives prepared, then choose the best three as the exam approaches? The criteria for assessment for all grades are printed in *These Music Exams* – a useful source of reference for teachers.

A:1 Corelli *Sarabanda*

Many pupils enjoy the expressive qualities of minor keys, so this delightful dance movement should prove a popular and rewarding choice. In selecting the piece, however, bear in mind that there is a fair amount of movement around the keyboard, especially in the left hand.

During initial practice, when breaking the piece down into its component parts, the pupil will benefit from understanding the binary-form structure (with phrases either two or four bars in length). Smooth finger changes are needed for the right hand's repeated notes in bars 9–12, and the second finger on B♭ in bar 11 might be an easier option. Ornaments, although not obligatory, would be expected in order to gain high marks; when fitting them in, care should be taken not to distort the pulse.

A mixture of detached and slurred notes will give lightness and elegance to the rhythm: detaching the crotchets in bar 1, for instance, complements the slur in the following bar. All left-hand octaves may be detached, thus helping the smaller hand.

In the right hand the player should aim for an expressive violin-like tone, and thinking one-in-a-bar, lightening second and third beats, will avoid lumpy accents on each note. At bars 14 and 15, however, feeling the crotchets in pairs will help to characterize the hemiola.

A:2 Hässler *Moderato in C*

The inverted counterpoint of this piece, with its two main seven-bar phrases, will fascinate any pupil interested in how music is constructed.

Playing a succession of accidentals may be new to your pupil, but the patterns in bars 1–3 with their mirror-image fingering (reversed between the hands in bars 8–10) fall comfortably under the fingers – provided that they remain close to the black keys. Elsewhere, the fingers need careful organization to encompass all notes reliably.

Although only two dynamic levels are indicated, examiners will appreciate musical playing that responds to the shape and direction of each phrase. Thinking towards the first beat, perhaps with a gentle crescendo through each sequential figure, will give a feeling of progression through the opening three bars, and the pupil must decide whether or not to keep growing towards the *forte* at bar 8. The ending may be played either *forte* or with a slight tailing-off in bars 13–14.

The staccato wedges, representing the same as the more familiar 'dot', need clarity to bring the phrasing to life. Slurring is marked in bars 1–4 and 8–11; elsewhere, there must be differentiation between the staccato crotchets and held notes, which will require good hand independence. The right-hand C in the final bar is tied, the staccato instruction simply indicating that both hands finish exactly together.

A:3 Mozart *Allegro in F*

One can only marvel at the five-year-old Mozart for producing such a delightful and well-crafted piece. A few fingering manoeuvres, especially in the left hand, will need careful practice, but the repetition of ideas within the ternary structure means that there are only six bars of notes to learn!

A two-in-a-bar feel will be conveyed by lightening the offbeat quavers, and there must be no hesitation between sections at bar 4. Using the third finger in the right hand at the start of bar 4, as suggested, may prove easier to control than the thumb; however, your pupil will need to shorten the dotted crotchet in order to allow time to move up to the C.

Thinking of the opening four bars as one phrase, with a rise in tone towards the third bar, will give shape to the melodic line. In the middle section your pupil may have to work to project the 'echo' effect suggested by the dynamics (playing *piano* confidently can be difficult in the early grades); a slight diminuendo in the first three notes of bars 6 and 8 will add graceful nuance.

Although only a few staccatos are marked, detaching the quavers in the outer sections will immediately establish rhythmic buoyancy. Contrast is provided by the slurred detail of the middle section. Here, the semiquavers may be slurred through to the following quaver, though care should be taken to avoid stressing the first (offbeat) note of each group.

A:4 Kress *Menuet*

This charming dance with its attractive melodious right-hand shape has straightforward rhythmic patterns and a reassuring absence of black notes. Although its movement is largely scalic, the left hand may need separate practice in order to negotiate the leaps confidently.

Moderato suggests an unhurried tempo, which will allow the music to flow in a gentle, graceful manner. Phrases are either two or four bars in length; clear legato with no overlap of the fingers is essential to create smooth lines in both hands. A gentle crescendo towards the middle of each four-bar phrase in the first half will give shape and momentum, with care taken to round off each phrase with a diminuendo. The second half offers the opportunity for an echo effect at the repeated phrase, and the suggested left-hand staccato at this point is effective if articulated clearly.

Balancing the two hands is a skill that pianists need to develop from the earliest stages, so practice and careful listening are required to project the right-hand melody over a lighter left-hand accompaniment throughout. Playing with the right-hand thumb very close to the keys in the bars with repeated notes (e.g. bar 4) will highlight the upper melodic line. A slight ritardando over the final two bars will help to bring the piece to a gentle close.

A:5 Krieger *Menuet*

With its subtle interplay between the hands, this minor-key Menuet is among the most beautiful examples of this popular dance-form when played sensitively. A good sense of keyboard geography is needed to negotiate the leaps securely, but the virtually identical repetition of bars 1–8 at the end makes the piece relatively straightforward to learn.

Crotchets need even spacing at an unhurried tempo, and care should be taken to fit in the rhythmic detail at bars 5, 14, 16, 21 and 22 without distorting the pulse. Playing cadential trills as eight equal semiquavers starting on the upper note may be an easier option than the printed suggestion.

Imagining the treble and bass texture as a duet between two instruments may help in understanding the phrasing. The overlapping lines at the start require independence between the hands in order to show clearly the phrase endings (or musical 'breaths'). In contrast, bars 5–8 (and elsewhere) can be played as one long phrase. Clarity of fingerwork will help achieve a good legato. At the octave stretches smaller hands may lightly detach the notes.

Well-shaped cantabile tone with no sudden accents will contribute to the gentle character. Pupils should also be aware of the subtle change of mood at the C major middle section.

A:6 Türk *Carefree Happiness*

This cheerful piece should bring a smile to even the most anxious pupil. It also serves as an introduction to ternary form, having a dominant-key middle section and a da capo (to be played). Two, not four, beats per bar must be conveyed, so the tempo chosen must be lively – but *Poco allegro* warns against attempting an over-ambitious speed.

Clear dynamic contrasts, often not well executed in an exam, will characterize this jaunty style. There should be an audible differentiation of levels in bar 4, and the second section from bar 9 onwards will be more shapely if the tone drops back at bar 13 to allow a crescendo to the cadence of bars 15–16.

At both loud and quiet levels, fingerwork requires control and evenness. Slow practice will be needed to ensure that the hands play exactly together in bar 1 (and similar).

Each phrase begins with an anacrusis (an impressive word for any pupil to know!), so there is always a feeling of upbeat momentum towards the first beat of the bar that follows. Playing the quavers staccato gives rhythmic buoyancy (those marked in the score should receive slight emphasis), but it is simpler to play the left hand's dotted figure smoothly to match the right-hand semiquavers in bar 1 (and so on). An implied ritardando in bar 17 will prepare the pauses before returning to tempo.

B:1 K. J. Bischoff *The Industrious Student*

Any hardworking pupil will be inspired by this title, and the appealing melody is encouraging too. This piece has the advantage of sitting comfortably in two hand positions: the first, in A minor, from bars 1 to 8, the second – at the change to C major – from bars 9 to 16, then returning to the A minor position from bar 17 to the end.

In this lilting piece the right hand is always to the fore, but care should be taken not to exaggerate the accents. The smooth phrase that ends in bar 2 with a lift of the hand on the B is followed by a gentle drop of the hand onto the E, avoiding a bump in the line or a hard sound. Those accents that occur in both hands together are no more than an opportunity for expressive leaning into the notes, rather like a tenuto marking.

In bars 8 and 16 the dotted minims must be held for their full length so as not to cut the phrases short, and a breath should be taken before continuing with each of the following sections.

For a smooth, even-quaver accompaniment in the last section (from bar 17), a rocking side-to-side motion from a flexible wrist needs to be used, and in the last bar the quavers should slow gradually to wind the music down.

B:2 Enckhausen *Andante*

There is the potential for the anxious candidate to set off too fast here, only to come to grief in bar 3 with the quaver movement. Encourage your pupil, therefore, to think through the first line before starting to play. This is advisable in any performance, but especially so in an exam when performing pieces of different styles and tempi. It is not unusual for examiners to hear three pieces played from start to finish all in one tempo!

This deceptively simple piece is quite complex and sophisticated for the grade, needing hand independence and ease of flow. The notes do not fall easily under the hands, so plenty of separate-hand practice will reap huge rewards, especially if the performance is musically considered and incorporates shading in the phrasing from the outset.

The tenuto markings on the crotchets in bars 1, 2, 9 and 10 require emphasis, with slight separation between notes, and using the finger pads for a warm sound. This will also highlight the imitation in the part-writing. The accent in the left hand in bar 7 should not be overdone, but played with enough weight to give sufficient singing tone to carry over the bar-line. Otherwise the touch is mostly legato, and fingering needs careful consideration in order that quavers are smooth and even.

Pupils will enjoy the final crescendo and diminuendo, which bring the piece to a satisfying close.

B:3 R. Fuchs *Banges Herzelein (Sad at Heart)*

Not all pupils will respond to the melancholy feeling in this music, but the piece is a gift for the musical student. A flowing tempo and the ability to make the right hand sing are the ingredients for a convincing performance.

The right hand needs to be legato as well as cantabile, so would benefit from being learnt separately at first. There is a danger of producing unwanted accents on the notes following tied dotted crotchets (e.g. the B in bar 1), and your student should avoid letting the hand fall onto these notes.

The left hand's broken-chord figures could be practised initially as solid chords, to feel the shape of the harmony under the hand. Once the shapes are mastered, the broken chords – gently accompanying the melody – need a light touch aided by a loose arm and wrist. If the pedal can be reached, the direct pedalling marked will give a bloom to the sound; an effective performance, however, is quite possible without pedal.

Although few dynamic markings are given, there should be rise and fall within the phrases throughout. Who could fail to enjoy the moment in bar 11 when the right hand reaches for top C, the highest note in the piece? This provides the dynamic climax from which to fall down to a beautiful *pianissimo* at the end.

B:4 Blatný *Allegretto*

This cheerful little piece requires independence of the hands, with the challenge of a staccato touch in the right hand and a legato touch in the left. There are, however, only two hand positions involved: the C major position and the G major position.

A gentle hand staccato – a little pecking motion in the hand, up and down from the wrist – will achieve lightness in the right hand. For smoothness in the left, the wrist should be rocked gently from side to side between the chord and the single note (played by the thumb), the fingers kept firm.

In addition to the marked articulation, consider a slur from the quaver E of bar 16 through to the first G of bar 17. The left hand's V marking in bar 24 is a reminder to lift the G but hold the F underneath – enabling a slur to the E-G chord in bar 25. The last C in the right hand needs enough tone to sing through to the final bar's pause, but too forced a sound will lose the sense of the end of the phrase (and the piece). Care must be taken to strike the left hand's last chord quietly to avoid overpowering the right-hand C.

The catchy melody of this 'musical nursery rhyme' will make it an appealing choice for the young Grade 1 student.

B:5 Köhler *Melody*

This lilting Melody comprises eight four-bar phrases. It has a one-in-a-bar feeling, which your pupil should aim to convey. A good right-hand cantabile and balance between the hands are also required.

Separate practice of the right hand will enable its melodic shape to be understood. The accented C in bar 3 and similar is only a slight emphasis, the wrist dropping in a slow downward motion but with the fifth finger firm and supported. The following note should be played carefully so as to match the sound of the dying accent.

Enjoy playing the piece with your pupil as a duet, taking turns on the melodic line and the accompaniment. Concentrating on one hand at a time will encourage awareness of the balance between the parts. Another option is to shadow play (or mime) the left hand while playing the right with full tone.

To achieve a singing melody line, the repeated As in bars 1 and 2 should be held for as long as the note-length indicates, and let go at the last minute before replaying. The left-hand stretch in bars 26–7 when reaching down for the E♭ is tricky. Practise this with the left hand alone until ease of movement is built in.

Dynamics are well set out, but add a small rallentando at the end and the melody will fade away musically.

B:6 Loeschhorn *Study in C*

Those students who find reading the bass clef difficult will delight in a piece written entirely in the treble clef, the left hand playing in the piano's middle range. The left arm will therefore be positioned across the body throughout. (Do not suggest a shift nearer the top end of the keyboard as the pupil may forget to move back again!)

The element of study here is keeping the fingerwork even in the right-hand quaver movement while maintaining a flowing circular motion in the left hand. The touch is mostly legato, and the right hand's slurring in bars 1 and 2 should not be too clipped – more like violin bowing than piano slurs. Grace notes should be light, without any clumsiness or accentuation. Your pupil should first practise the melody without the acciaccaturas, adding them later with a light flick of the fourth finger.

Dynamics are detailed, but you might add a crescendo from bar 7 leading to bar 9's *mezzo-forte*. Bars 13–16, which repeat bars 9–12 exactly, offer the opportunity for an echo effect, the dynamics this time at *piano*. Allowing the last two bars to taper off with a diminuendo will avoid an accent on the final unison C.

Choose a tempo with which your student is comfortable, and encourage breathing space between the four-bar phrases to ensure a poised and neat performance.

C:1 N. Bachinskaya *The Old Cuckoo-Clock*

This is an excellent study in staccato playing, the right-hand articulation conveniently consistent throughout!

Allegro moderato suggests a pace that is appropriate for less experienced fingers. Crotchet = *c*.120 seems a sensible tempo, which probably needs no modification, apart from at the pause. In fact the pause can be quite substantial, to convey the music's humour and pictorialism.

A useful preliminary drill for the right hand is to practise below speed, on any two notes, playing from the fingertip and a well-curved first joint. Immediately after striking the key, the finger can be pulled rapidly inwards towards the palm and, once the two fingers are co-ordinated, the player will both sense and see a 'running' motion. Where the thumb is needed, the edge can be used and the release from the key will be upwards rather than inwards. For the best effect, movements should be contained and economical.

There are three dynamic levels marked – none of them loud – in addition to a crescendo and hairpin diminuendo. It would be best to leave most of the diminuendo to the last bar, so as to avoid anticipating the dynamic point of arrival.

You may need to explain what a cuckoo clock is to some pupils, and stress that the mechanism of this one is clockwork and not digital!

C:2 Michel Le Coz *Mini Rag*

The appealing ragtime flavour of its music will surely make this piece a popular choice.

In the first half, the left-hand part needs to be firmly rhythmic, almost march-like, and a free arm and wrist motion behind a strong fingertip staccato attack will establish the music's rhythmic character. The gentle emphasis, requested in the second half, can be achieved by a very slight separation of the notes. Crotchet = *c*.144 (as mentioned in the footnote) works well, and no tempo alteration is necessary at any point.

As an alternative to the printed fingering, you might try using 3-3-2-2-1 for the treble notes in bars 9–12, and 1-2-3-4-5 for those in bars 13–15. The more complex rhythms of right and left hands in these bars may be clapped in a teacher–pupil exchange to help accustom your pupil to the irregular division of the bar.

Broadly speaking, the piece's first half is loud and the second half quiet. The hairpin crescendo from bars 10–12 should probably peak at *mezzo-forte*, so as to avoid stealing the thunder of bar 16's *forte*.

Examiners sometimes hear swung styles played straight and vice versa. Remember that the quavers here are straight, not swung, and that the da capo needs to be included.

C:3 David Sawer *Moebius*

This gentle, atmospheric piece is likely to appeal to those temperaments attracted by a more ascetic soundscape. The music's rocking motion evokes a barcarolle, and the metronome mark of dotted crotchet = 68 yields exactly the right sense, while guarding against musical loitering.

The piece is legato at all times: the hands can be kept close to the keyboard, fingers poised in readiness. Melodic material is passed from one hand to the other, and your pupil needs to be aware of balance, imagining that one arm is slightly heavier than the other at appropriate points. The dynamic is mostly a restrained *piano*, and the crescendo needs careful grading so that too much is not given too soon, especially as the *mezzo-forte* does not signify any great climax.

It is unlikely that pedal will be used at Grade 1, although a simple, legato pedalling, changing with the bar-line, will work throughout. Tone control from the fingers, rather than from the foot, is more important at this stage.

And why not present your pupil with a puzzle? Consider the relationship between the left hand's notes from the second half of bar 4 to bar 7 and those of the right hand from the opening to the first half of bar 4 – then find out all the other relationships of this sort!

C:4 Alan Bullard *Flying above the Clouds*

'Graceful and dreamy' instructs the copy – and this piece should suit a pupil who also fits this description!

Although both hands play in the treble clef, the notes are easily encompassed; those in the right hand lie mainly adjacently while those in the left are triadic. The touch should be legato throughout, ensuring that notes at the end of phrases are held for as long as possible but without being gracelessly emphasized.

The dynamic need not rise much above *mezzo-piano,* but the sound will benefit from a cantabile firmness – since evenness of touch and flow are paramount considerations. Although the joint of the first finger must not collapse, there should be a feeling of contact between the fleshy pad of the finger and the key.

The piece presents an ideal opportunity to introduce some simple, regular pedalling (pupils can't wait to get their feet moving down below!). Because the action involved is one of direct rather than legato pedalling, fingers and foot engage and release simultaneously. Thus, just after the finger plays the second note (and beat) of bar 2, the pedal is raised and as the finger depresses the first note (and beat) of bar 3, the pedal is likewise depressed. In bars with dotted-crotchet, quaver patterns, the pedal may be raised as the quaver is played, and so on. At the very end the sonority is allowed to accumulate as our dreamer drifts off into the next cloud.

C:5 Elissa Milne *Skedaddle*

The piece's title is certainly appropriate because, taken at crotchet = 176, the music really dashes along. However, crotchet = 162, although less headlong, yields a perfectly acceptable pace.

The swung rhythms and 'bluesy' right-hand part make this an attractive option but not an easy one, as it demands a secure knowledge of each hand's keyboard geography. The right-hand part is limited to five pitches, which can be practised independently at their lower and higher octave positions. In bars 7 and 19 the thumb may be used on the E, if replacing it with the third finger causes confusion. The left-hand part is probably more complex, the chromatic passages requiring special attention.

Care with the changes of register will be needed in bars 14–15 where, to locate the relevant hand positions, the focus of attention must pass swiftly from right to left hand and back again. Concentrating on the note E will provide a 'signpost'.

For a fully stylish performance, attention should be paid to contrasting articulations, and your pupil needs, as early as possible, to assimilate the sensation of implementing two contrasting actions simultaneously. The piece is a nineteen-bar crescendo (with a sly left-hand *piano* thrown in at bar 15), which needs careful judgement. Done well, this cumulative effect will bring a Grade 1 programme to an exciting conclusion.

C:6 Lionel Salter *Frogs*

In this good-natured frolic, the musical skips could be thought to portray leaping frogs or even children's leapfrogs. Whatever picture you have, choice and manner of articulation are likely to be important in conveying the music's character. The staccato touch needs to be a genuine finger staccato, crisp and from the very tip of a well-curved digit.

A tempo of dotted crotchet = 108 is ambitious although manageable by a fluent Grade 1 player, but anything down to about dotted crotchet = 90 will preserve an appropriate two-in-the-bar feeling. Stability of pulse is important, however, and no ritardando is necessary, even at the end, because its application might weaken the humour of the music.

The fingering is straightforward and the notes lie comfortably under the hands. Perhaps using repeated thumbs for the two Es of the right hand in bar 10 is a more straightforward option than changing 2-1 and, in bar 13, the notes repeated at a lower octave may helpfully be taken by the left hand.

Examiners will appreciate a good dynamic palette, ranging from a full – though not percussive – *forte* to the final *pianissimo* (which may be aided by the *una corda* pedal). The dynamics are 'terraced' rather than nuanced but your pupil will need to practise and memorize the sound and sensation of five different levels!

GRADE 2

Lessons will have been learnt from Grade 1, and pupils will probably want to play something similar to their favourite piece from the last exam. The pacing of the preparation, not forgetting the supporting tests, will probably be easier with the experience of Grade 1 safely in the past.

A:1 Haydn *Allegro*

Students enjoy playing in the key of G major. It is a bright key, which suits the brilliant and bubbly character of this movement. The piece is a good example of ternary form, and as such gives only sixteen bars of music to learn! The left hand's octaves from bar 13 may be impossible for younger pupils to stretch, but just the top line (or the bottom if preferred) can be played alone, so long as the sound is still strong. Note that the dynamic markings are editorial; whatever dynamic structure you choose to follow, however, the pupil should in addition create rise and fall within the phrases.

As the metronome mark suggests, the piece should have a one-in-a-bar feeling. Quavers in the right hand might be lightly detached to give clarity. The left hand needs careful control: firstly, do check that the treble clef has been observed before any study is done at home; secondly, the left-hand thumb in the semiquaver patterns should be light, and a little rotation in the wrist will keep the notes even. Building this into the technique from the outset will avoid tension later.

This cheerful piece has broad appeal and will be a popular choice.

A:2 Löhlein *Balletto*

The 'ballet' of the title is not referring to classical ballet but rather the earlier type of ballet that was more akin to a comical spectacle. This piece is jaunty and rhythmic, with a slight emphasis on the first beat of the bar. The tempo marking of *Allegretto* suggests vitality and energy, but that the tempo is not too fast.

The ornament at the close of each section might cause difficulty, yet if it is incorporated into the line from the initial stages of learning it should not interrupt the flow. The instinctive musical candidate will give just a tiny breath before putting this inverted turn on the beat.

The 3rds in the right hand will present a technical challenge to players at Grade 2; with a firm bridge in the hand and curved fingers, the notes will sound clearly together.

Guard against the opening *forte* being heavy and overblown, since too weighty a sound will obscure the grace and charm of this style. A diminuendo in bar 7 might enhance the overall shape of the first section, and an additional *forte* in bar 13 would brighten the return to the first theme before the piece fades away at the end, the performers of the ballet disappearing off-stage.

A:3 L. Mozart *Bourrée*

The bourrée is usually described as a rapid dance in two or four, beginning on the upbeat. This elegant example is given a cautionary tempo marking of *Moderato*, though the buoyant two-in-a-bar pulse should be felt throughout.

Care must be taken that the left hand's chords do not drown the right hand in the first phrase (and where it repeats). In fact, to maintain a light texture the balance of the hands should be addressed throughout. The more gifted student can be encouraged to join the bass line of the left hand's first chord progression (while lifting the thumbs to replay the Bs), thus adding an extra touch of polish to the performance.

The listener must be able to hear that the phrases are two bars long, and also the 'question and answer' dialogue between them. A light touch is needed for the repeated notes at the end of the first phrase, and similar.

The corner at bars 11 and 12 is awkward for the right hand. In order that the chord shapes may be managed easily, the passage may need repeated practice; it will further help if these bars are memorized.

This was among the pieces that Leopold Mozart composed for his young son Wolfgang Amadeus to perform in concert – an inspiration for your pupil, perhaps!

A:4 Handel *Air (Hornpipe) in D minor*

This stylized jaunty little dance is deceptively tricky due to the contrapuntal nature of the writing; it involves some jumping to find notes, so would be best for the pupil who has a confident command of the keyboard.

The key to success lies in a bold touch and good hand co-ordination. Playing the left-hand notes slightly detached throughout will achieve a stylish effect – the touch *mezzo* staccato unless the note-length exceeds a crotchet. A variety of articulation in the right hand will bring the music to life. Consider slurring the first-beat semiquaver, quaver pattern, lifting the hand on the quaver. The syncopated figures that follow need a staccato on the quaver and a small accent on the crotchet in order to emphasize the offbeat rhythm.

Work out a dynamic plan, though it should be open to change as time goes on. Remember that examiners will accept any ideas, as long as they are musical. You might make a positive start with a *forte*, dropping to *mezzo-piano* for the sequence at bar 5. A further diminuendo to *piano* at the beginning of bar 8 leaves scope for a crescendo to reach a strong *forte* at bar 11.

This is a good piece to start the exam with. It needs to be spirited and positive in touch, and so will familiarize the player with the piano immediately.

A:5 Mozart *Menuett in B flat*

Your eight-year-old pupils will be amazed to learn that the child prodigy Mozart wrote this piece at their age. It is a sophisticated little dance, which will require careful preparation both in learning the notes and in organizing a reliable fingering.

Nearly all the slurring is editorial; if young players cannot manage the octave stretch in the opening bar, the two B♭s can be separated. The exception is the right-hand two-note slurs in bar 5: these are Mozart's markings and must be played. They can be achieved effectively by dropping the wrist on the first note of each group of two and lifting the hand up on the second note.

Repeated notes – in the left hand of bars 1 and 2, 9 and 10, 13 and 14 – are always a minefield for inexperienced players. Playing them with a slight stress on the first beat of the bar with two lighter notes to follow will avoid any heaviness and achieve a graceful style.

Fingering of the trills in bars 4, 12 and 16 might be better with 2-3-2, since little hands may find 2-4-2 (or 3-4-3) rather difficult to co-ordinate. Likewise, in the penultimate bar smaller hands will find a third finger (rather than the fourth given in one edition) on the first D in the left hand easier to find.

A graceful appoggiatura at the end allows the dancers to bow to each other as the music comes to a close.

A:6 Türk *This Makes Me Want to Dance*

We have to honour the title here and ensure that the playing does make the listener want to dance. The suggestion of *Non troppo allegro* (not too fast) is a wise one, because this is a piece that could easily gain too much momentum and lead to the dancers falling over.

This light one-in-a-bar piece jumps around a lot, needing agility and even fingerwork. The pupil must watch out for the change of clef for the left hand at bar 17 (the right hand also moves position) as well as the held Ds in bars 21 and 22 – they give a dominant pedal effect and must be heard. Firm and supported fingers are required in the right hand throughout. The spread arpeggio at the beginning of bar 5 is stretchy; if young players cannot reach all the notes comfortably, the bottom D of the chord may be omitted. A quick sideways motion (the hand peeling the notes off from the thumb to the fifth finger) should be applied when rolling the chord.

The marked dynamics might be further enhanced by a diminuendo in bar 7 to finish bar 8 at *mezzo-forte.* Then start bar 9 *forte* with bar 11 a contrast at *mezzo-forte,* returning to *forte* at bar 13.

In order to indicate the pause over the double bar-line at the end, the player should be still before breaking the atmosphere and going on to the next piece.

B:1 Sarauer *Grandmother's Tales*

Everybody enjoys a good tale, and this piece of musical storytelling – with its questions and answers, climax and gentle ending – provides limitless fruit for the imagination. Although there should be a little rhythmic flexibility to breathe life into this expressive music, the quaver detail needs careful spacing and the minims at the ends of phrases must not be hurried.

Initial practice without pedal will develop the finger legato essential for a good cantabile line. Releasing the keys efficiently in the left hand (especially the thumb notes) ensures clean harmonies. Note, however, that the thumb A is held throughout bar 7.

Use of the pedal will provide truly smooth chord changes, especially in the final four bars (even though the piece can be played without). By developing the skill of listening critically the pupil can ensure that the pedal releases clearly when each new harmony sounds.

Singing the phrases at a convenient pitch will help to establish the song-like character. Although the predominant marking is *mezzo-forte*, there is scope for considerable tonal inflexion, especially at the ends of phrases. The climax occurs over bars 7–10, where the left hand adopts a more sonorous and supportive role. The ending needs a well-graded diminuendo – and all chord notes should sound, even at the quietest level.

B:2 Krug *Der Kuckuck und die Nachtigall (The Cuckoo and the Nightingale)*

This attractive piece, which portrays both the call of the cuckoo with its familiar falling 3rd and the high-pitched nightingale song, should prove a popular choice with sensitive, imaginative candidates.

It falls into three main sections, the first and third of which are identical, and, although there are a few changes of hand position to negotiate, the chords generally fall comfortably under the hands. The tempo, while conveying two beats in a bar, should be unhurried, with rests given their full value. Moving from quavers to semiquavers at bars 4, 16, 18 and 22 needs careful judging – and making a slight ritardando in the second half of bar 18 will ease in the final section.

Saying the word 'cuckoo' – with its slight emphasis on the first syllable – will help shape the opening calls; a crisp, light staccato is needed here. The contrasting slurs should be articulated clearly, lifting the fingers efficiently to prevent any blurring of sounds.

The middle section, beginning at bar 9, becomes more impassioned, with the left hand assuming a more important role. The right hand's 3rds in bars 10 and 12 need careful practice to ensure clarity, the thumb being released in time for the same note to be replayed by the left hand. The gentle appearance of the nightingale at bar 15 is a lovely dramatic moment, which requires sensitive tonal control.

B:3 Rowley *The Bee*

In this delightful piece, with its gently buzzing figuration shared between the hands, one can readily imagine a bee travelling from flower to flower in search of pollen. Although it is a cleverly disguised study for developing evenness of fingerwork, the piece should have an unhurried tempo – suggesting a warm sunny day in which any movement quivers almost imperceptibly.

Practising the trill-like figuration separately will help to ensure evenness of tone and rhythm among the fingers of both hands. Players should explore the full dynamic range, and further gentle rising and falling of tone within the two- or four-bar phrases will give a natural musical shape.

The accompanying quavers should always serve, not overpower, the semiquaver line; careful listening will ensure that the hands are neatly co-ordinated (bars 17–24 may be particularly troublesome). Slurring from the first to the second quaver of the accompaniment and lightly detaching repeated thumb notes will help to give the all-important one-in-a-bar feel. At bars 29 and 31 the tenuto chords should be given their full length and slight prominence; elsewhere, however, any accentuation should be almost imperceptible in order to preserve the gentle character.

The performer may choose whether or not to slow down in the final phrase; it would be effective either way.

B:4 R. Fuchs *Wiegenliedchen (Cradle Song)*

Musical pupils who can shape phrases sensitively should enjoy the challenges of this attractive lullaby. The suggested metronome mark will allow the piece to flow, provided that the rhythm has some elasticity; thinking two-in-a-bar will prevent too many stressed beats.

The piece may serve as an introduction to legato pedalling, a vital ingredient for sustaining harmonies and creating a rich texture. Often the harmony changes twice in a bar, requiring only two pedal changes, but bars 7–8, for example, will need a change on every beat. The confident pedaller might explore partial use of the pedal, lifting at the ends of phrases to 'let the air in'. The pedal action on an unfamiliar piano can cause problems, but the ear should be used as a guide to achieve a clean harmonic texture.

Fingering should be chosen with care for ease of movement; some left-hand patterns in particular will need separate practice.

The dynamic range is small (*mezzo-piano* to *pianissimo*), and the right-hand line, supported by a carefully balanced left hand, should be played simply but with gentle rise and fall as dictated by the melodic shape. Subtle voicing can be explored in bar 1 when the G of the tune tucks into the left-hand chord, and quiet thumb notes will ensure that the upper melody projects in bars 11–12.

B:5 Kabalevsky *Little Song*

This charming piece is in the style of a minor-key folksong. With its simple yet evocative harmonies and gentle melodic contours, it will appeal to sensitive, imaginative pupils who can shape lines and balance the tone between the hands. Singing the melody at a convenient pitch, possibly adding words, will help to grasp the piece's melancholy character.

The accompanying chords should be practised separately in order to achieve good legato and clear synchronization. Bear in mind that there are several ways of fingering the left hand at bars 9–14 if the shifting thumb movement seems unnecessarily complicated. In bars 3–4 the player must hold the tied G while releasing the lower notes, and in bars 5–8 a short 'breath' at the end of each right-hand slur will highlight the phrasing.

The main climax of bar 12 is followed by a *subito piano* (no diminuendo to spoil the effect). Elsewhere, natural dynamic inflexion, as if singing, will give shape and interest to the melodic line, and care should be taken over the repeated notes to avoid 'bumping' the line. Throughout, the tune and accompaniment are at different dynamic levels and this must be conveyed – good balance is required even at this early grade. The *Broader* indication for the final three bars implies both a relaxing of the gently moving but unhurried tempo and an increase in tone.

B:6 Sandré *You Can't Catch Me!*

The title describes perfectly the character of this witty piece, with its unpredictable twists and turns, and it is best suited to a confident pupil with well-developed fingers and a strong sense of pulse.

A hazardously fast tempo is not necessary for a convincing performance but the crotchet pulse must be rock-steady (there will be a temptation to rush the semiquavers and the rests). Bars 7–8 may be particularly prone to rhythmic distortion; initial practice of these bars omitting the triplet will establish a firm rhythmic framework.

Producing the light, deft touch appropriate to the character may be problematic for some candidates, especially on an unfamiliar piano. However, control can be improved by working on scales or a finger-exercise at *piano*, *pianissimo* and *pianississimo* levels, always playing confidently to the base of the key to ensure that every note sounds.

The main climax is reached at bar 17, but gentle dynamic inflexion along the way will give direction and shape to the performance. Chords from bar

9 onwards should be carefully balanced to support, not overpower, the melodic lines. The clearly marked phrasing should be sprightly and alert; the grace notes (to be on or before the beat according to choice) need clarity. The pause at bar 19 offers a moment of repose before the music finally disappears.

C:1 John McLeod *The Temple by the Sea*

The exotic image conveyed by the title is poetically reflected in this atmospheric, compelling piece. Although the harmonic language may be unfamiliar, it might remind pupils of their atonal improvisations when first exploring the piano's sonority. They didn't always think of musical pictures in major or minor keys!

While the piece may be played without pedal, it will be more musically rewarding if pedalling is used, either as marked or beyond this. Try depressing the pedal before playing the first chords – the resonance from the undamped strings will create a mysterious start.

A relaxed yet weighty fall into the keys will help to give a reliable and soft tone in the right hand. The left hand at the start will need a much more focused attack, using a rounded hand and weight behind the fingers for a cantabile tone. Dynamically shaped phrases are vital to convey the mood.

All jumps will need preparation. The playing of the chord in bar 13, for instance, is the 'trigger' for a swift move straight to the melodic notes. At the end of bar 16 the comma should be taken literally: a compelling silence, in which pedal can be added, or changed, before the next bar. A similar effect at the end of bar 24 will enable the dramatic *subito piano* that follows.

The final bell and gong should not be rushed; instead, enjoy the resonance as the image fades.

C:2 Donald Waxman *Close to Danger*

This piece is aptly titled in more than one sense. First, there is drama in every note, the understated yet menacing left-hand melody adding tension while the right hand's quiet energy hints at the underlying threat. Secondly, performance of the piece is not without danger. Unevenly articulated semiquavers will spoil the effect, and the left-hand jumps over the right in bars 10, 11 and 12 are potentially unsettling.

Technical work in the right hand will pay dividends. Bringing out every second note, working in triplets or short 'sprints' in fours, for example, will all help control. When putting hands together, focus on just one bar (e.g. bar 2); slowly then with increasing speed, try to acquire evenness and quietness in the right hand while communicating a clearer tone and articulation in the left. In bars 4 and 5 similarly, the left hand's dynamic shape needs to be encouraged, the legato carefully controlled.

The left-hand melody should be significantly to the fore but within a generally *piano* dynamic. Getting the balance correct is crucial to a convincing performance, and the control needed for this can only come from slow, musical practice. Towards the end it is important to achieve a *pianissimo*, so as to give the sforzando final note dramatic impact.

This is an extremely effective composition, and attention given to the musical detail and good control will reap rewards.

C:3 Pam Wedgwood *Garage Sale*

Performances of popular jazz/rock-style pieces can lack an idiomatic feel and understanding of the rhythmic patterns underlying the pulse. Listening to some rock music with particular reference to the 'push' on the second and fourth beats as well as the emphasis on syncopated figures will help, but for best results the performer should play along to a rock drum pattern. This could be on an electronic keyboard, sequenced on computer or even using 'household percussion' (e.g. slapping the hands down on a cupboard top and an upturned saucepan).

All couplets should be approached from above the keys, dropping for a solid, but not forced, accent and lifting for a lighter end. In bar 1, for instance, the second and third beats should be exactly this; the penultimate quaver thereafter is short and light before a relaxed drop onto the final quaver of the bar.

The performance will only have conviction if articulation, rhythmic energy and dynamics are there throughout. The contrasting middle section presents a more legato and melodic right hand (interrupted by the left hand's bold rhythm section), but momentum must be maintained. A musical feature should be made of the crescendo in bar 15 (starting *piano* will enable this); there is no ritardando but a 'fade out' in the final bars before the abrupt 'distorted guitar' final chord.

C:4 Paul Bowles *Oh! Potatoes They Grow Small over There*

One of the more bizarre titles in the syllabus, it nonetheless relates very well to the piece. Not only does it convey the melancholy of a small potato spending a miserable existence underground but the words of the title also fit exactly to the opening phrases.

A true legato touch, and listening to the overlap of the notes, is needed to convey the first left-hand melody; a low wrist and fingers close to the keys will give the weight behind the tone. Small breaths between phrases will help ensure that rests are observed, and well-described dynamic shaping will enhance the vocal nature of the tune.

The left hand moves around, so all leaps need to be anticipated – the hand moving early enough to avoid any unwanted emphasis. This is particularly true in the final six bars. The right-hand 3rds in bars 19–20 should be as legato as possible; some practice releasing the previous notes a little after the next have sounded will reap huge rewards for future grades! The 3rds should also be quiet to avoid interfering with the melody. Finally, encourage your pupil to use a bold dynamic range throughout and to make the final three notes quiet but slightly separated, thus showing the accents.

C:5 Peter Maxwell Davies *Snow Cloud, over Lochan*

Having lived for over thirty years in Scotland, it is inevitable that a Scottish theme should pervade Sir Peter Maxwell Davies' compositions. Some comparison with bagpipe tunes and even other Scottish-influenced pieces by Maxwell Davies would introduce pupils to the imagery of Scotland and the rhythm of the 'Scotch snap'.

The piece itself needs a spacious calm and no angularity of tone. The melody should have a gentle shape, with all marks of articulation interpreted within this context. The rather unusual staccato markings under the phrase lines do not indicate that the notes are abrupt or accented but just gently released, the first semiquavers of the snaps slightly emphasized. The smooth waters of the lake in the left hand need to be unruffled, poised in tempo and beautifully legato, so some careful fingering will need to be considered – particularly in bars 17–23 (where the minims must be held under the crotchets) and through the 3rds in bars 10–15. Thoughtful listening to the overlap of sound and release of the previous notes will help the control and develop a true legato.

To support the calm image of the snow cloud the tempo should be unhurried and steady, and the dynamic level varied smoothly and consistently. The *poco rit.* of the penultimate bar leaves a slightly elongated rest as the cloud leaves the lake and the F major chord reveals once more the flat, clear surface.

C:6 arr. Jenő Takács *Satirical Song*

Charm, playfulness and a wicked humour are infused into this song with its rather jeering melody and deliberately teasing irregular phrases. Most of them are three bars long but the occasional two- and four-bar phrase keeps listeners on their toes.

The opening two phrases are clearly a question and answer, the left-hand melody a little quieter than the melody in the right hand that follows. For the contrast in dynamic to be properly expressed, the accompanying chords must be kept out of the way. Balance plays a crucial part throughout the piece.

Equally important will be a firm rhythmic precision, which the articulation will highlight; to help the character, tenuto marks should be deliberately yet not heavily defined and all slurs followed. Fluency will be helped by thinking ahead; anticipating mentally the jumps of hand position before reaching the ends of phrases should ensure quick yet relaxed jumps (at, for example, bars 3–4 in the right hand).

The *Presto* at the end – a playground jibe before running off – also needs some preparation in the mind, both to establish the tempo and also the staccato touch. The wrists should be relaxed to allow a quick bounce into the key, and there should be a small 'breath' before the placed final chords with perhaps a touch of pedal for warmth.

GRADE 3

Perhaps it is time to be a little more adventurous in the choice of pieces, now that exams are quite a familiar experience. Something of quite a different style might broaden the pupil's outlook, so do explore the alternative pieces as well as the printed selection.

A:1 Purcell *Hornpipe*

This attractive, spirited Hornpipe needs to be approached with the rum-filled boisterousness of a galleon of sailors. It is not fast, but energetic, with rhythmic vitality, charismatic phrasing and a strong left hand. Examples of the Hornpipe abound, so encourage the dance's character early on by having your pupil listen to other examples.

It is the left hand that should, perhaps, be approached first, as there are many tricky corners. All long notes should be sustained for their full value both under and over moving crotchets. Changing fingers on a note while sustaining it (such substitutions occur in, for example, bars 5 and 8) will probably be a new skill to young pianists, and one that is important to learn.

Many of the crotchets work best if detached and light, the more robust steps of the dance being saved for the minims and semibreves. This will also help avoid some awkward stretches such as the leap of a 10th in bar 1.

A buoyancy and 'spirit' to the melody will come from clear articulation of the excellent editorial slurs and by giving each phrase a decisive dynamic shape. The first and second phrases aim for the decorated dotted minim in the second and fourth bars, their final notes shaded gently to provide a feminine ending. The third phrase is four bars long, and the intensity should be sustained across the middle two bars to give the contrasting length of line.

The melody's buoyancy will be enhanced by some simple ornamentation. Although the editorial realizations work well, consider simplifying the ornaments in bars 2 and 4 by using the realization suggested in bar 12. Ornamentation makes for a stylish performance, but should be omitted if continuity is affected.

The editorial dynamics are very effective and will add colour and interest.

A:2 D. Scarlatti *Larghetto*

This wonderfully expressive, slightly plaintive piece will delight and entrance both listener and player. It is deceptively simple, for there is much to consider musically; its charm and beauty could easily be lost in the wrong hands.

Balance plays a vital part in conveying the melody; the left hand should be gentle and legato or, if preferred, very slightly separated on occasion – which will give a lightness of touch, thus 'lifting' the dance character. Small 'breaths' in the left hand, matching the right hand's phrasing, would be very appropriate between bars 9 and 10, for example, and perhaps between bars 6 and 7. However, here we meet the enticing dilemma of exactly how to phrase the attractive melody.

The slurs are not necessarily to be taken literally. Does, for example, the opening bar descend in a legato line to the first beat of the second bar, or is the first bar itself a small phrase with its own identity, a small breath being given at the bar-line? Although both ideas can work very effectively with the right dynamic shading, bars 9 and 10 seem more obviously to be separate entities. The couplet phrasing (the composer's own) in bars 6 and 7 can be played literally, provided that due weight and length is given to the first note of each couplet.

The player must take care not to rush the ornaments, which should be melodic and shapely. A carefully considered and controlled use of dynamic is essential for giving the exquisite melody poignancy throughout, right up to the beautiful E♭ in the penultimate bar.

A:3 Türk *Allegretto*

This delightfully naive piece has little of musical depth but much in the way of technical fun and games! For the more physically confident and well-coordinated pupil it may be a rewarding choice.

The opening eight bars are relatively uneventful, the phrases needing only dynamic shape and light, feminine endings. But after the double bar-line the left hand leaps over the right with speed (yet delicacy) to play what is effectively a counter-melody. Here a quaver rest helps the jump to be achieved – provided that the hand moves as soon as the crotchet D is finished. The jumps are best practised by 'shadow jumping', stopping on the first right-hand D after the double bar and checking that the left hand is already covering the F♯. Similarly in bar 10, time should be taken to ensure that the right hand has covered its D as soon as the left hand has played the second of its giggling top Ds.

The right-hand jump in bar 12 is much harder, and within a *pianissimo* dynamic the hand's speed of movement may result in an unwanted accent on the bottom D. A little ritardando through the latter part of bar 11, however, works well musically and will herald the return of the opening idea. Similar practice is needed in the following bars, but the player must look out for the altered rhythm in bar 21 where many a performance may slow. The semiquavers should be lightly tucked in despite the *forte* dynamic.

The performer is wise to go no faster than is indicated by the excellent editorial tempo marking. The notes, as the composer suggests, should be caressed, and the piece kept gentle and unflustered right through to the closing *pianissimo*.

A:4 Handel *Menuet in G minor*

Originally a fairly lively dance, with couples moving in the shape of an 'S' around the room, the Menuet soon developed into something a little more refined and slow. This poetic, graceful Menuet is definitely one of the slower, more poised of dances and is beautifully tinged with the sadness of a minor key.

In its apparent simplicity lies its difficulty: what to do with all those left-hand quavers, and how to phrase the melody? This is naturally at the player's discretion, but so much of the character will be lost without eloquent articulation. The right-hand quaver, crotchet rhythmic figure of the opening bar (and bars 5, 7, 11; notice too its subtle introduction into the left hand in bar 16) lends itself to a shortened light quaver and a slight lean into the crotchet. The same rhythmic feature in bar 2, this time in the second half of the bar, is more of a written-out appoggiatura, and might be more legato and expressive with a slight lift just before the E♭.

The left-hand quavers of the opening work well if gently detached. There are degrees of 'detachedness', though; subtly separated notes can be just as effective as very short ones. In bar 2 the first two notes of the left hand might be slurred together. The rest of the left hand could be variants on these detached and phrased ideas. This will require some independence between the hands, and the necessary control will be achieved with separate practice.

Dynamic contrast and shading will also enhance the musical interest. Consider a *forte* in bar 9 and echo in bar 10, for example. Elsewhere, make sure that complete phrases always have shape.

A:5 Mozart *Allegro in F*

This jolly Allegro bubbles along in the form of a lively dance. Its repetitive nature will aid learning, but makes it all the more important to convey the musical interest – subtle dynamic shading of the melody, balance between the hands and dynamic contrast.

Firstly, decide on the right-hand fingering in bars 20–21. Starting the demisemiquavers with 2-1-2 will make the transition smooth and bring a lightness of touch. Consider also using this fingering at the beginning (a nice 4-3-2 fingering then follows) and elsewhere. But whatever the fingering, small, slightly less assured fingers may struggle to control the demisemiquavers. The pupil should practise resting the fingers on the surface of the keys, then use just the fingers to control the scale slowly – not lifting the non-playing fingers unless employing the 2-1 fingering, in which case thumb moves under second finger. Gradually speeding up and using a little more finger should give the desired evenness.

This piece's grace and charm could easily be destroyed by heavy left-hand 3rds and by a lack of subtlety in the melodic shading. Quiet, relaxed staccato chords will help achieve a good balance; the wedge-shape staccatos are interchangeable with staccato dots so do not need a brighter tone. In the right hand's repeated notes (e.g. bar 1), grade the dynamic away from the first note, then lean into the crotchet of the next bar with a pliant wrist and a slight placing of the note. Elsewhere, accenting first beats should be avoided, and runs (such as in bar 5) approached with a light hand, making a crescendo towards the first beat of the next bar.

A small ritardando at the end is perfectly permissible, with the triplets spread evenly through the quaver beat to the final curtsey.

A:6 Telemann *Aria*

This poetic aria is quite seductive in its apparent simplicity. A closer look, however, will reveal its unusual phrase lengths, which give the piece an expressive inventiveness and great subtlety. The perfectly balanced first phrase, ending in bar 3, is barely three bars long, yet it seems only natural that the following phrase is four-and-a-half bars. This second phrase is extended by beautiful interjections, inspired thoughts along the way.

Make the most of the song's vocal nature by giving beautiful dynamic shape to the couplets (effectively written-out appoggiaturas) and tender feminine ends to phrases. Note that the couplet slurs to the semiquavers do not signify a shortening of the second and fourth notes; they relate to string bowing, which means legato lines are called for. Other right-hand quavers, such as the opening note and the first bar's second beat, can be lightly detached.

In the left hand, a poise and elegance is maintained by slightly detaching the crotchets and quavers, though a more legato approach could work if co-ordination proves difficult. Either way, the left hand should be light and not in any way intrusive, the melody being sensitively shaped.

Two corners may prove unsettling. The first is the demisemiquaver figure, which should not be snatched. The second is the ornament (the small cross, in bars 8 and 14), which should be an expressive melodic turn.

Finally, exploit the absence of dynamic markings in the music. Encourage your pupil to come up with ideas, and then try them out until happy with the performance. If the musical ideas are the pupil's own, they are far more likely to be convincingly expressed.

Lightly detached final quavers and a placed, poised final note will end the Aria with charm.

B:1 C. Franck *Chant de la Creuse (Song from the Creuse)*

Creuse is the name of a river in central France, and the folksong style of this charming melody will be immediately apparent. It starts with a simple statement of the first theme, the hands an octave apart, which is then harmonized. Notice the unequal phrase-lengths and the different time signatures – care must be taken not to short-change the 3/4 bars.

The slurs indicate where notes and chords should be joined and where tiny 'breaths' are desirable. Although it is easier to join the chords using pedal, at Grade 3 not every pupil is ready for this. The challenge, then, is how to achieve the required legato without pedal.

It takes effort to make repeated notes sound smooth, but if the opening theme is sung to sol-fa names (soh, soh, doh, doh etc.) one can hear the legato line being slightly punctuated by the consonants, *s* and *d*. In trying to imitate this on the piano, each finger must 'cling' to the key, allowing it to rise just enough for it to be replayed. This should be felt as an arm stroke, rather than hand or finger movement.

Joining the chords needs careful fingering, especially if managing without pedal. However, so long as the melody notes are legato, the occasional gap underneath can be disguised, and taking some right-hand notes with the left will help. From bars 21–4, for instance, if the left hand's G and B♭ are played with fifth and fourth fingers, the thumb can play D and second finger the E♭ and C♯ of the inner right-hand line. The E♮ that follows should stay with the right hand. This kind of fingering is second nature to the organist, but is vital for the pianist too, and well worth mastering for future use.

B:2 H. Hofmann *Waldvöglein (Little Woodland Bird)*

Over the centuries birdsong has inspired countless poets and composers, and this beautiful woodland scene is sure to be a popular choice. Here the trees are still, hardly a breath of air rustles the leaves and, overhead, a little bird is singing.

Each hand has a distinct and contrasting role to play. The left hand creates a mood of peace and solitude while the right plays the part of the bird, singing his heart out as he flutters from branch to branch. Why does the piece sound sorrowful? Is it the bird or the listener who is feeling so sad? Let your pupil decide.

Begin by learning the left hand, practising the notes of each bar in block chords first so that the outline of the harmony is understood. It quickly becomes apparent where there is repetition and where there are significant changes. The hand should be relaxed and as still as possible, the fingers close to the keys. The dynamic level remains at *piano* or *pianissimo* with a little more tone on the sustained dotted crotchets, especially as they move downwards in bars 5–7 and 25–8.

The right hand, picking out the rhythmic mottos, melodic fragments and chirping of the little bird, is altogether more mobile. The opening dotted-note figure should always be crisp, and the recommended finger changes will help to keep the articulation clear. In bars 9 and 11, take the acciaccatura and quaver figure in one movement, striking the notes almost simultaneously and allowing the hand to tip towards the little finger.

The slurs, legato lines and staccato should be carefully observed, as should the effective *rit.* and pause just before the last phrase; make the listener wait and wonder what is going to happen next.

B:3 Kullak *Die Wanduhr (The Clock on the Wall)*

Clocks have long been associated with music, and even before the invention of the metronome, composers have been fascinated by mechanical rhythm. The song *My Grandfather's Clock* and Haydn's so-called 'Clock Symphony' immediately spring to mind, and in the eighteenth century pieces were even written for mechanical clocks.

As with all music imitating machines, this amusing little piece will depend upon really strict time. Once it is 'in the fingers' (even while still at a slow tempo), no harm can be done by practising it with a metronome! The player must keep count of quavers with every appearance of the main tune; it would be so easy to leave some out, especially when feeling nervous in the exam room.

A crisp staccato will be essential, and at the separate-hands stage it would be wise to develop a secure left hand. The chords in bars 9–12 are very awkward, and the *ossia* or alternative version is strongly advised for all but those with a very large stretch. Only a few groups of notes are marked to be played legato. The semiquaver figures almost all begin with an accent that should be incisive but not heavy, and the chords in bars 13–16 marked with slurs need to be as smooth as possible to contrast with the general spikiness of the piece.

Everything that a convincing performance requires is written in the score – the lively tempo (*Allegro vivace*), dynamics, accents and articulation marks. If these are conscientiously observed, the rhythm and tone are even, and there is no technical tension, success is assured.

B:4 Kirchner *Allegretto, poco agitato*

The tempo indication *Allegretto, poco agitato* immediately gives a clue to the character of this exciting piece. The offbeat accompaniment, syncopated figures and moments of repose, amid a general sense of urgency, all suggest a game of running then standing stock-still. If you so much as twitch a finger in the pauses before the music resumes, you are out!

The right hand's quaver chords are best thought of as staccato, and while at first they are heard merely as accompaniment, from bar 9 they assume a more significant role, marking the rising harmony and tension. In the left hand of bars 1–4, playing the pairs of notes together will allow the ear to notice how the diminished 5th chords resolve onto the 3rds. This will help to determine melodic shape. The tricky cross-rhythms of bars 5 and 6 will benefit from some separate-hands practice. An increasingly agitated left hand is firmly restrained and put into place by the right hand as the first pause is approached.

Interestingly, the pedal markings indicate that the left hand's upbeat quavers are sustained to create a distinct bass line for the texture. This pedalling is not difficult so long as there is a prompt release on the quaver rests. If your pupil is not yet ready to use pedal, a similar result can be achieved by holding the upbeat quaver under each crotchet. (Indeed, this happens in bars 5 and 6.)

Dynamic marks should be followed carefully. Remember, too, that for exam purposes the first-time bar should be omitted, the player moving smoothly into the last four. Here a well-timed rallentando will help to negotiate the shift onto the cadential chords.

B:5 Maikapar *A Passing Thought*

This delightfully elusive piece is ideal for the pupil with imagination. The way that the composer depicts his subject – using melodic fragments, repetition, held notes and even silence – will provide opportunity for some lively discussion.

Notice that the piece is to be played *leggierissimo* with a dynamic range of *pianississimo* to only a little above *mezzo-piano*, so lightness of touch and nimble fingers will be required. Slurs and staccato notes are all scrupulously marked, and note-lengths should be carefully observed. For instance, in the left hand's staccato figures (from bar 5 and from bar 13) give the crotchets a little more length than the quavers. The phrasing is clearly indicated by hairpin marks, which should be regarded as nuances rather than significant changes in volume. Examiners are often startled to hear huge and sudden increases in volume (*piano* to *fortissimo*) when a small crescendo mark appears, instead of a slight swelling of the tone.

The left-hand melody starting in bar 17 may require extra work. If necessary, try out different fingerings for the slightly awkward manoeuvring needed as the passage moves downwards; it must sound as agile and rhythmic as the previous right-hand figures.

A touch of pedal can help sustain the dotted crotchets that close almost every four-bar phrase (it will not be difficult to apply, so long as your pupil can reach the pedals comfortably). The whole bar of silence also gives time to depress the *una corda* pedal for the final two phrases. This will provide another shade of colour, and help to create the impression of the 'passing thought' disappearing into thin air.

B:6 Mendelssohn *Romance*

The aptly named *Romance* will appeal to those who enjoy sentimental music. A mood of nostalgia contrasts moments of regret with thoughts of happier times.

The first theme has two distinct ideas: a figure of falling 4ths in a dotted rhythm, then a balancing phrase of a smoother, more flowing shape. The dotted-note patterns, while remaining rhythmically accurate, should not sound jerky. You might like to sing the words 'long ago' or 'far away' to help both rhythm and mood. In the middle section, from bar 9, the dotted rhythms can be livelier as the music moves into the more cheerful major key.

The staccato quavers in bar 3 should not be too short; elsewhere they are marked with a slur, and probably should all be the same. Accompanying chords need to be placed gently so as not to obscure the melody line, but notice that they are not always of the same length.

The mood brightens at the increased dynamic level in bar 9. Feel the rise and fall of the phrasing and aim for a very smooth left hand. With the repeat of this four-bar phrase the tone is more subdued, and a harmonic change in bar 16 introduces an extra two bars to round off the phrase. Here the dotted-note figure is less confident as it sinks sadly back into G minor, and a slight ritenuto would be effective. In the two *pianissimo* closing bars, let the descending 'cello' notes sing, while keeping the accompanying chords as quiet and sustained as possible.

This is an excellent piece through which to learn about form and phrase structure, as well as being musically satisfying to play.

C:1 Bartók *Round Dance*

This wonderfully spacious piece, a favourite for many teachers, encourages the development of rubato, and a well-projected cantabile sound.

It will help if the player can 'breathe' with the music, and feel sufficiently relaxed to have a real physical freedom across the keyboard. The left hand's widely spaced chords need to be found with ease, and pedalling is essential to produce a smooth connection between them. If your student cannot reach the pedals comfortably it would be advisable to choose another piece from this list, since pedalling is such an important ingredient here. In fact, additional legato pedalling would enhance the playing of the repeated notes in bars 6, 8 and 18, and would allow more time to find the chords in the tricky corner at bar 16.

The swells of the crescendos and diminuendos are mostly over two bars, giving two-bar phrases except for one longer four-bar phrase (from bars 7 to 10).

Expression marks should be followed closely as they are the composer's. Do watch that the *pianissimo* in bar 9 is maintained into bar 10, and then that the right-hand crotchet C♯ is played very quietly indeed so that the semibreve E can still be heard above it. A little time should be taken over this bar before easing back into the reprise of the melody, which this time has a change of harmony. A tiny 'breath' before the first chord of bar 13 (played *piano*) will allow the moment to be savoured, adding that touch of magic to this expressive and haunting gem.

C:2 Giles Swayne *Ice-Cream Van*

It is exciting for a young person to play a piece by a living composer, and this descriptive piece provides an excellent introduction to contemporary music. It will suit the adventurous pupil who has a good sense of rhythm; also essential is the ability to control and count fully the long notes and rests.

Although quite complicated on the page at first glance, the piece can very quickly take shape upon analysing the patterns and repetitions of motifs. It would be wise to learn it in small sections which are then slotted together rather like a jigsaw puzzle.

The opening motif represents the chimes of the ice-cream van and occurs four times – each time a little louder than before. It must be played with care, for the last two crotchets of the first bar could easily be miscounted as a crotchet and quaver (making the pulse an equal 6/8 instead of 7/8).

The semiquavers in the right hand of bars 3–5 need clarity. Repeated in a one-bar pattern, they represent the chugging van heard in the distance. In bar 39, the semiquaver pattern returns, the van starting on its journey home then disappearing away back over the horizon.

The middle section (bars 14–27) is slightly faster and perhaps depicts children scurrying to the van to buy their ices. It must sound busy, as the composer indicates; the right hand, entirely on white notes, and the left, on black, require a bouncing touch. Tempo I is retaken at bar 28, where care must be taken to play both hands in the bass clef.

Overall this is a very effective piece, which because of its vivid imagery would be a suitable item for a school concert.

C:3 Terence Greaves *Bonny Bobby Bluetoe*

Jazz-style pieces are always popular with candidates and this one will be no exception. A swing version of the nursery rhyme *Bobby Shaftoe*, the piece moves at a swift tempo and needs confidence and precision at the keyboard.

In order that the title's swaggering character is conveyed, the dotted rhythms will be most appropriately executed in a lazy jazz style rather than in exact dotted-quaver and semiquaver groups. The tempo indication of crotchet = *c.*168, bouncy, is quite brisk; the footnote recommends instead *c.*144, which seems more manageable at this Grade.

The grace notes in the left hand to begin with (and later in bars 9 and 11 in the right hand) should be lightly squashed into the crotchets, avoiding any heaviness or slowing in the pulse to accommodate them. The first two beats of the right hand in bars 9 and 11 should be played lightly to convey the *delicato* marking that the composer gives here, and watch that the left-hand accompaniment in bars 9–12 remains staccato and *pianissimo.*

Halfway through bar 14 the rhythm takes a different turn, and this corner will need a lot of practice before pupils can feel their way around the syncopated pattern with ease. Fingering of the left-hand chord at the beginning of bar 15 (G and B♭) may be easier as 2/1, for then the hand is in the correct position to play the next chord of C and B♭.

Pedal is suggested in places, and if legato pedalling is used, it will help sustain the tied notes in the penultimate line. The *una corda* marking in bar 17 (not to be missed) lifts at bar 21, and the piece concludes in the same easy-going way as it started, finishing with a cheeky accented chord.

C:4 Martin Butler *Evening Bells*

I can remember as a child the thrill of staying up late into the evening in the summer holidays, the light fading – and hearing the sound of church bells pervade the air. This piece no doubt conjures up for many such a nostalgic image, and it will appeal to students who are able to sustain concentration, given the potential here for losing one's place on the score, or counting incorrectly. It is a sophisticated piece and will be best assigned to an imaginative player, whose range of pianistic colours will be broadened as a result.

Your pupil needs to have both a good sense of keyboard geography and the ability to move across the keyboard freely. Being able to reach the pedals is essential also, since the bells would not be able to ring without the inclusion of the sustaining pedal. Be sure to lift the pedal on striking the last chord in each phrase (as the composer has requested), so that there is no resonance during the sounding of that chord.

Reading leger lines will present the most problems initially, and until those notes are built in to the memory bank, general fluency will take time to come. Counting is the other challenge; it may be advisable to learn this piece in chunks, a few bars at a time, and then piece it together rather like a jigsaw puzzle.

The marking *sonore* in bar 14 suggests that the bass E and C should have more weight and tone. This is in imitation of a deep bell, the sounding of which gives a sense of finality to the piece.

C:5 Grechaninov *A Frightening Experience*

Written by one of the great Russian composers of miniatures, this charming piece provides the perfect opportunity for inventing a narrative with your student, telling a ghost story along the lines of 'One dark night …'. The wide dynamic range and changes of tempo will help the student to characterize the tale.

Notice that tempo changes are sometimes gradual as in *poco accel.* and *rall.* (which should not be too exaggerated), but at other times are immediate shifts of pace – as in *Meno mosso* and *Tempo primo.* There are musical surprises along the way, which will allow players to develop their interpretative ability. The harmonic palette is rich, and further tone can be created by putting the sustaining pedal down on the dotted minims with pauses.

The melody is shared between the hands for the first phrase (in the left for the first bar, moving up to the right for the second). The answering second phrase (bars 3 and 4) is completely given over to the left hand. The melody should be practised alone before adding the accompaniment, so that the ear is used to hearing the direction of the melodic line.

The accompanying repeated chords in the right hand require a light touch, with a bounce to the wrist (keeping it relaxed) – the fingers gently nudging towards the back of the keys on the chord replay. Point out that the right hand's chordal progression from the last beat of bar 4 until bar 8 is chromatic. Feeling the notes under the fingers and working this out away from the copy can make the passage less daunting.

This fun piece is likely to be popular with candidates. It might also be a good choice for concerts and festivals.

C:6 Nikki Iles *Willow*

There is much to enjoy in this contemporary piece. With its lazy offbeat accents and expression, it will suit the youngster who enjoys playing in a relaxed style and who is able to feel the beat instinctively.

The falling melody line of the right hand, representing sighing and melancholy, depicts the branches of the weeping willow swaying in the breeze. The art lies in giving sufficient warmth to the tone on the tied dotted minims, to keep the sound alive while avoiding an unwanted accent on each first beat. The use of arm weight – the weight being transferred across the keys from the quaver upbeat to the dotted minim – is essential for the long phrases to sing. When the melody is presented in 6ths from bars 8 to 12, some judicious fingering is needed to maintain the legato line. Substituting fingers will help, changing the top fingers from 4 to 5 on the chords in bars 9, 10 and 11.

Direct pedalling simultaneously with the left hand's accented chords will add a certain bloom, though while depressing the pedal the player should guard against overemphasizing the left-hand chords due to the downward motion of both actions. In addition, the temptation to bring in the chords early must be resisted, so that the rhythmic impetus of the syncopation can be felt throughout.

This beautiful, lyrical piece needs meticulous counting to be fully effective, but it is certainly rewarding and will be popular with performers and listeners alike.

GRADE 4

Many of the List B pieces will benefit from some pedal, but if legs are too short there is always an alternative piece from the extensive lists. The musical character of candidates often becomes more firmly established at this stage and they can play to their strengths, making sure the pieces are contrasted in tempo and mood.

A:1 J. S. Bach *Prelude in F*

Bach's little Preludes have provided generations of aspiring keyboard players with an enjoyable way to develop their musicianship and finger technique. Among the simplest of the collection, Prelude in F is nevertheless a joy to play: it lies comfortably even under small hands and its regular semiquaver rhythm weaves attractive, uncomplicated patterns.

As a general rule, lightly detached quavers, sustained crotchets and crisply articulated semiquavers work effectively throughout, and will create a bright, clear texture. There are just a few spots that might cause awkwardness if not given some preliminary practice. If turned into little finger exercises, these corners will flow comfortably and feel familiar when they are returned to the complete phrase.

The first 'exercise' is bar 2 played to the first beat of bar 3. Isolating this serves to prepare the change from fifth to fourth finger on the E in the right hand, and to cultivate a seamless join in the semiquavers as these move from right to left hand.

The second is bar 4 to the start of bar 5. Here the left hand has a similar finger change, then must negotiate a shift across the keyboard down to the low F. This should be as smooth and even as possible.

A third exercise is from the middle of bar 12 to the middle of 13. The right hand needs to move forwards a little into the keyboard in order that the fifth finger is comfortably positioned for the B♭s.

The suggested metronome speed and dynamic marks work well, but remember that little nuances within the given dynamic level can highlight the shape of the phrasing and create more colour and expression.

A:2 Hook *Air*

This delightful piece by the English composer James Hook is light-hearted and musically uncomplicated. In order to convey this bright mood in the style of the early Classical period, most of the quavers should be played with a lightly detached touch and the longer notes sustained. Later, some of the quavers may be slurred for expressive purposes, as in bars 17 and 18 (and again in 21 and 22) where slurring the left hand creates a more tender mood. Similarly in bars 25 and 26 (also 29 and 30), where a hint of B minor briefly casts a shadow, slurred quavers in both hands could highlight this darker colour.

The right hand will need careful practice in order to synchronize the pairs of notes cleanly. A light touch of pedal may help to join the slurred chords in bar 2 (and similar), by depressing the pedal on, or just after, the first beat, and letting it up cleanly on the second. If bar 8 is treated the same way, the left-hand semiquavers must be kept quiet to avoid a smudge or bulge in the sound.

The cadential trill at the end of each section may well cause difficulty as it leads directly onto a chord. The trill could be reduced to a group of six notes (sextuplet), or even four (in effect a simple turn), but whatever is decided, the last two notes must be A and B, and every effort should be made to move smoothly and in time.

Elsewhere there are few problems, and the recommended metronome mark gives for a stately, unhurried pace. A slight ritenuto through the final cadence will make a positive statement to round off the piece.

A:3 Zipoli *Preludio*

Preludes of this period are often of an improvisatory nature, and this is no exception. While much of it flows along with a steady underlying beat, it should not feel too strict, and there are places where the harmony requires time and space to make its mark.

A very expressive piece, it will require careful fingering for the part-playing to be sustained and balanced musically. Notice the beautiful descending sequence that begins in the treble (minim F♯) at bar 3 and then passes to the alto with the last quaver of bar 6. At bar 12 it is the turn of the bass, joined by the tenor at bar 14. However, bear in mind that long notes – as with those in the treble at bars 12–15 – need a little help to stand out against a moving part. These are heard as suspensions, with the harmony moving underneath, and should resolve gently onto the following quaver – the hand then lifting so that it can drop into the next long note.

A harpsichord player would almost certainly arpeggiate some of the chords, either for expressive purposes or to negotiate them more comfortably; examples are the dominant 7th chord beginning of bar 10, the two chords in bar 45, and each section's final chord. In bars 22–5 just drop into the ornaments on the second beats – don't try to connect them to the preceding notes.

The harmony is rich and expressive throughout, but the most remarkable moments occur in bars 32 and 34, where the anticipated tonic notes of perfect cadences are flattened by a tone. This extraordinary effect needs a little extra time to avoid sounding wrong! The music should then resume a steady pace, slowing down a little before the final cadence.

A:4 G. (J. A.) Benda *Presto*

J. A. Benda was from a distinguished family of musicians, originally from Bohemia and active in Germany during the eighteenth century. This Presto is reminiscent of a tarantella, and its brilliance will make it popular with those who enjoy playing lively music. A metronome mark of dotted crotchet = *c.*120 will give excitement without too much danger.

A few tricky moments could become permanent trouble-spots if not dealt with early on. The first two bars, while looking innocent, require reliable fingering before the lure of increased speed, especially as the bars are repeated several times. If the given fingering seems fussy, try the fourth finger on E both bars, but use consecutive fingers in bar 2, ending with the thumb on B; in bar 3, meanwhile, use the fifth on the tied F, resuming with the printed fingering at bar 6.

Some of the left-hand quaver figures will need extra attention to achieve the agility of those in the right hand. It will help to practise the broken-chord figures (bars 20–26) initially as block chords. Not only will this help establish good fingering, the harmony will be better understood. At bar 27, care needs to be taken over the F♮, which, given the various accidentals in this passage, might be played as F♯.

The pedal marks are unusual in this edition – the pedal is to be released cleanly on the x sign. These touches of pedal, although not entirely necessary, do help, especially with the trills.

A:5 Handel *Allemande*

The cheerful, buoyant mood of this Allemande is hard to resist. Its crisp rhythms and stately tread conjure up scenes of courtly ballrooms and royal processions. Listening to some of Handel's most popular works – *Music for the Royal Fireworks* and *Water Music* – will help to develop a sense of style, and the recommended Associated Board edition clearly shows how to tackle the characteristic Baroque rhythms.

The principal melody is in the right hand, and for the most part a bright, detached touch is appropriate; the even semiquavers in the second half of bars 6 and 15, and the quavers in bar 14, however, could be smoother. The left hand's typical harpsichord texture – the notes held and overlapped in order to fill out the harmony and enrich the tone – requires an altogether more legato treatment. There are, nevertheless, places where a detached touch could be employed, for example on upbeat quavers (fourth quaver in bar 1) and on quavers at cadences (first half of bar 6) – but this is purely a matter of choice.

Pedal is best avoided altogether to allow the sound to be clear and transparent, but there must be some changes of colour and dynamics. As a general rule, it is natural to make a crescendo as the music rises and a diminuendo as it falls; and in this piece, the return to G major at bar 12 is effective if played quietly, allowing for a build-up towards the end. Remember, though, that the left hand's descent through the octave at cadences should be tapered, and when the figure is in crotchets (bars 7 and 16) it should not be rushed.

A:6 Hässler *Allegro in E*

If energy and brevity are what you are looking for, this exuberant Allegro may well fit the bill. Lasting little more than half a minute, it lies neatly under the hands and is musically uncomplicated.

Typical of this period, the melody is constructed out of triads and scales, and the left hand provides a broken-chord accompaniment. Only the four-bar phrase beginning at bar 9 will require special attention – the semiquavers divided between the hands needing careful control to avoid unevenness and bumps. As a preliminary exercise, play both notes together in each hand. With the thumbs sharing the same note, the left hand should be slightly forwards and higher with the right hand positioned behind. Once this has been practised for a while, the melody line will emerge and the notes learnt more quickly. Then, keeping the fingertips fairly close to the keys, allow the hands to move freely from the wrist with each pair of notes. Very soon the passage will become confident and fun to play.

It is always useful to practise broken-chord figures as block chords – and to be able to put a name to the chords. This accompaniment must not become heavy, even though the opening passage is marked *forte*. The melody needs a bright attack and should move rhythmically without loss of speed into the semiquaver scale and crotchet chords of the cadence. Pedal can be used to good effect in the first four bars (changing every two beats), and on the final cadence. These last chords need to be counted carefully, as do the earlier minim rests.

Once in the fingers, the piece can be played with enjoyment and panache.

B:1 Granados *El fantasma (The Ghost)*

This is not the usual dance-style piece that we associate with Granados, but a descriptive piece suggesting an energetic phantom out on its night's work to scare people. Each of the first four phrases ends with sudden accented *fortissimo* or *forte* chords, which convey the shock of the unsuspecting bystander when the ghost suddenly appears. If these chords are memorized, the pupil can look down confidently at the keyboard, finding the chords without hesitation. The accented B♭ octaves in bars 2, 3 and so on are best highlighted by lifting the previous quaver and landing securely on the accents using some arm weight.

The middle section (bars 24–42) looks daunting, but closer inspection will reveal that the semiquaver arpeggio pattern in the right hand is almost identical across the four phrases; only the second has a different rhythmic shape (bar 28) and a slight change in notes at the end of the flourish (bar 29). Strong and secure fingers are needed here, with special attention paid to curving the fourth finger when passing it over the thumb. The left hand's tied chords in this section are likewise slightly different arrangements of the same harmony. To ensure accuracy of notes, it would be best to practise this section initially in blocks of two bars, before trying to link up the four-bar phrases and establish the flow.

The tempo in the last section is slightly slower and the touch more legato and expressively shaped. The now weary and docile phantom disappears into the ether to sleep for the day.

B:2 Grieg *Cattle-Call*

One can always rely on Grieg's music to stimulate the imagination of both performer and listener, and this pastoral folksong is bound to inspire pupils. The beautiful haunting melody line calls out for a good cantabile sound, and the balance of the melody and accompaniment should be keenly judged for the song to project clearly.

After the two-bar introduction, depicting the cattle-call in the mountains, the sicilienne rhythm of the main tune needs to be played with firm fingers. Keep the melody to the fore, with the underneath parts in the background and as legato as possible. This Allegretto section would certainly benefit from legato pedalling throughout (if the student can manage it), to give smoothness to the sound and to add colour. In bars 12 and 13 pedal would also assist with holding the left hand's chords – which for most young players will have to be arpeggiated.

As marked on the score, consider playing the long F♯ in the treble clef in bars 14–15 with the left hand at the top of the rolled chord. Then, immediately, take the same note (silently!) with the right hand and hold it, so that on the change of pedal with the left-hand bottom E, the F♯ continues to sing through the semiquavers.

In addition to the marked dynamics, consider a *piano* 'echo' effect in the triplet figure in bar 9. The final *pianissimo* will be very effective if the *una corda* pedal is used for the last four bars, where the contented cattle settle down for the night.

B:3 Sandré *Petits bateaux sur l'eau (Little Boats on the Water)*

This charming miniature barcarolle is a delightful sound picture, and imagery will play a big part in capturing the piece's character. The piece demands that students listen closely to the balance between hands, particularly in the opening section where the melody (in the right hand) and accompaniment are close in range.

The slightly choppy waters portrayed by the dotted rhythms need to have a lilting quality; that is, a two-in-a-bar pulse, not six quaver beats (as might be the case if the pace is too slow). Co-ordination of the hands in places is not easy, and time should be spent initially placing bar 2's right-hand crotchet E correctly between the left-hand dotted quaver and semiquaver. Inexperienced players could easily develop bad habits and put the E with the last left-hand quaver G♯. For the other tricky corners with similar co-ordination problems, have the pupil play one hand while you take the other, then reverse this process. This will be useful in developing listening skills, as well as being fun.

In the more spirited major section we lose the dotted rhythms and the waters become smoother. The right hand's acciaccaturas are best played before the beat and by light thumbs. Do not overlook the *rit.* in bar 24 – pulling up to let the passengers disembark – before the *a tempo* and *accel.*, when the children run out of the boats and disappear into the distance. The two closing chords should be cheeky and just lightly arpeggiated.

B:4 S. Heller *Study in A minor*

This dramatic and deservedly popular show piece will appeal to all ages, and it will encourage lots of good practice as it is tuneful yet full of drama. The term 'study' is not immediately appealing as a title, but there is always enjoyment to be had in Heller's brilliantly crafted studies.

Once the notes have been learnt, the main challenges are achieving equality of sound and evenness in the fingers. The triplets must dovetail seamlessly from one hand to the other (avoiding a bump on the entry of the right-hand thumb) – to sound as if played by just one hand. Practising the triplets in one hand alone will, in fact, help the student hear the desired evenness of tone. The triplets drive forward onto the minims at the end of each phrase, and the right-hand staccato chords lightly fill in the harmony each time. When developing evenness in the fingerwork, do not underestimate the value of slow practice both in the beginning and later on in the learning process.

Pupils with small hands may prefer to use the fifth finger in bars 25–7 at the beginning of the right hand's descending figures, for greater control, and may also leave out the right hand's bottom A at bar 31 and other octave notes where bracketed.

The direction *risoluto* for the last section suggests firmer fingers, yet the last *agitato* must be smooth without accentuation. Inexperienced performers should guard against the temptation to run away too much towards the end. The last two chords must be placed exactly in time to give a cheeky ending to this flashy piece.

B:5 H. Hofmann *Scherzo*

This is a Scherzo for which the title's usual meaning (a joke) is not entirely appropriate, and a more playful and whimsical rather than humorous character should be stressed. This sketch would suit the nimble-fingered and requires the student to be able to multitask with ease. (The metronome mark of crotchet = *c.*72 seems appropriate.)

The first four bars serve as an introduction. From bar 5 the melody in the left hand leads the way in a legato phrase, with the right hand's light and floating accompaniment above. The hands then swap roles for the middle section, and back again for the last, before the right hand has the final say from bar 37.

A common observation by examiners is that pieces and scales need more musical shape. Here is an opportunity to encourage students to shape the melody line with rise and fall within phrases. The introduction's two phrases each have a crescendo to *sforzando* – the sound here is to be warm, not fierce. The melody at bar 5 needs a slight rise to bar 6 before falling away to bar 7. Care must be taken, however, to avoid the phrasing becoming too exaggerated or bulging in sound.

Fingering is generally well-marked, but bar 18 may benefit from some reorganization. The right hand (on top E with the fifth finger) could also take the left-hand third and fourth semiquavers (F and A) with first and second fingers respectively, leaving the left hand free to play the first two semiquavers (G and B) before lifting to find the quaver G.

A delicate and charming piece, it will be a gift for the musical candidate.

B:6 Kullak *Eröffnung des Kinderballs (Opening the Children's Ball)*

Young players who like dancing and dressing for an occasion will enjoy the glamorous scenes conjured up by the title. One can imagine the girls and boys in pairs, making circles and patterns on the floor as they dance.

In the style of a polonaise (a robust formal dance), the opening repeated notes announce the beginning of the ball. The first dance starts at the upbeat into bar 5. This rhythmic and elegant first section leads into a smoother, more feminine dance from the upbeat to 13. The change of key into B flat major at bar 29 denotes another episode, perhaps with the boys escorting the girls on their arms in a courtly fashion.

The tempo should be fairly steady, with a strict sense of pulse. The repeated quaver as in bar 4, however, may slow down slightly before tempo is resumed with the upbeat semiquavers into the first dance.

Repeated notes are often problematic, especially on an unfamiliar piano. Candidates may try the piano on entering the exam room, and may wish to test the opening bars of this piece within that preparation time to see how the touch responds. Suggest to the player a bouncing action in the wrist, while changing fingers – as if bouncing a ball in the hand.

The stretch in the bass line in bars 13, 14 and 15 calls for some agility in the left hand; in each bar an alternative fingering is 5-2-1-2-1-2 if the thumb can be used neatly as a pivot.

This attractive piece, offering lots of contrast, will be fun for all ages.

C:1 Bjelinski *Alarm*

This piece is wonderfully descriptive and visual in its energy and purpose. The alarm of the title seems to imply the hustle and bustle of an emergency situation rather than the noise of a bell. To convey the character, therefore, think in terms of clean articulation, brisk tempo, and a strong rhythmic identity.

The editorial metronome mark works well if the articulation is clearly defined, staccato crisply executed and balance sensitively judged. In bars 13–22 in particular the right-hand semiquavers should be light with a latent excitement, despite the *forte* marking. In confident hands, a slightly faster tempo can be attempted, giving the performance slightly more sweep and drama. Ultimately, however, the ideal tempo is the speed at which the pupil has good control over the middle section's semiquavers, which are so exposed from bars 15 to 19.

In the outer sections the opening figures should be played exactly as written and with a one-in-the-bar feeling. The right hand's couplet phrasing will be achieved with a drop of the hand onto the chord, a pliancy in the wrist, and a lift on the subsequent note to keep it short and light.

The small dynamic details have a real significance. Starting the left hand's semiquavers in bar 7 quietly, for instance, will help effect the crescendo through the notes and increase the sense of urgency. At other points the left hand needs to have a confident independence, its notes short and to the fore.

The performance should be entirely rhythmic throughout; there is little need, if any, for a fluctuation in tempo except perhaps for a slight holding-back across the final two bars. So much of the piece's character will depend upon an organized and disciplined response to this particular emergency.

C:2 Bill Readdy *Bop Goes the Weasel*

Not just another of the many jazz-style pieces on offer, *Bop* exudes a real idiomatic flair as well as an infectious sense of fun. A potentially popular piece, and deservedly so, it will need more than enthusiasm alone, however; both an informed, innate jazz feel and a subtlety of touch are required to do it justice. Foremost will be the flawless sense of rhythm needed in the more upbeat passages. Dotted-quaver, semiquaver rhythms should be swung and, particularly from bar 17 to the end, the pulse kept strong and decisive.

From the outset the pulse must be clearly set and felt; jazz musicians would probably count in out loud here, so a '1, 2, 3, 4' in the head will help establish a clear tempo. Time can be taken in the cheeky, rather smoochy bars at the end of the opening phrases (bars 3–4, 7–8 and so on), and the pauses here could be 'milked'. A pupil might use pedal to achieve a legato between the chords, not just where marked but between each of the preceding chords.

Bars 16–20 will reveal the players who have really absorbed the idiom. In bar 16 there's an accent on the E, and it is this slight 'kick' on the swung rhythm's shorter notes that gives the 'feel' to the right hand and, overall, rhythmic life to the swung groove; the G♯ and following Ds in bar 17 require similar treatment. It may seem unnatural to make this emphasis, but practising swung scales will help. Couple this right hand with a positive and steady walking bass to create the buoyancy and energy needed, and make sure to hold the penultimate chord for its three-and-a-half swung beats.

C:3 Villa-Lobos *At the Bottom of My Garden*

This happy and compelling music – offering Brazilian sunshine and a relaxed, festival atmosphere – will provide musical reward in abundance.

Technically the piece is undemanding, with effectively only ten bars to learn – but much depends upon the chosen tempo. The editorial metronome speed may seem a little frantic; if so, consider crotchet = 68–76, to help characterize the left-hand semiquavers and give the folk melody greater charm. The left hand's stretch of a 9th may mean that this piece is not the most practical for those with small hands. At the same time, it is possible to redistribute this chord and play the first D with the right hand.

In bars 1–4 a positive tone to the right-hand top C is needed for it to last through two bars. The staccato marks on the semiquavers are rhythmic, implying precision without being too short.

One technical hurdle is to project the folk melody with clarity and shape, particularly in bars 6–10 where the right hand also takes some of the accompanying harmonies. Without a sense of balance, the texture will become cluttered and muddy, especially with pedal added. For the C major triad in bar 6, practise dropping on the G with the fifth finger and gradually introducing the lower notes. Once the 'feel' of achieving this balance is acquired, it will be a matter of shaping the melody with particular attention to the repeated Gs in subsequent phrases.

In bar 9 the left hand requires good independent control to promote evenly articulated and shaped semiquavers.

Pedalling plays a crucial role in creating the overall effect. Although only marked for the final two bars, it is implied in bar 10, and some passages cry out for pedal. Use it in the opening bars, for example, but consider leaving bar 9 dry to give bar 10 delightful warmth.

C:4 Alan Haughton *Baroque and Roll*

The humour in this tongue-in-cheek pastiche is not hard to understand, though pupils may not at first appreciate the joke. A quick look at something like No. 5 of the Six Little Preludes by J. S. Bach (BWV 943) may be needed.

The piece will be popular because of its jazz idiom yet it cannily provides the same technical challenges as found in Baroque music; it is therefore an excellent choice for developing independence between the hands. It is also particularly good for the more studious pupil, given that its best performance will be slightly understated, the articulation and dynamics played exactly as marked.

Although a meticulous sense of pulse is essential (as are evenly played semiquavers), it is in the detail that the piece's character resides. The lower notes of the right-hand semiquavers in bars 2–4 may be played as a hidden melody, to give vitality and musical direction – particularly if the articulation matches the left-hand quavers showing the offbeat emphasis. Small, bright and unforced accents in the left hand here and in the right hand of bar 10 will give these passages rhythmic buoyancy. The same type of accent on the first beat of 11–13, in addition, will idiomatically lead the crescendo to the *forte* at 14. A confident sense of the syncopation in bars 8, 17 and similar will also add the jazz seasoning.

Bold and quick (*subito*) contrasts of dynamics are part of the humour and should be exploited, particularly in bar 26. In this instance, though, care needs to be taken, as a reckless jump to the notes may result in a *forte* rather than the desired *pianissimo*.

The jazzy grace notes of bars 6, 8 and 14 should be lightly squeezed in with the 3rds, and consider a dab of pedal on the longer chords in bar 15 and the final bar.

C:5 Trevor Hold *A New Dance*

The title here is very apt – with a dual time signature the dance is new indeed, even surreal. But don't be deterred by the metric irregularity, as this is a characterful and comic piece, which will reward the effort put in. Once the counting is secure (this simply requires some aural work), the piece is fairly straightforward technically.

Begin by acquainting your pupil with groups of three and then two quavers to a steady quaver pulse, then different combinations of two and three. Finally, work at alternating bars of 3 + 2 and 3 + 3 + 2 – perhaps using simple percussion instruments until it can be 'felt', rather than counted, and the quavers experienced as a pulse of dotted crotchets and crotchets. Only after this should notes be hung to the rhythms.

Next, slow practice coaxing the fingering, notes and co-ordination into the hands is needed; finally – speed it up. The silver lining is that a fast performance is much easier and, at the recommended metronome mark (or faster), the piece really falls into place. Only bars 27–34 are technically demanding. Work on hand distribution is needed for the passage to sound fluent and even.

Some dynamic shape is needed across the two-bar phrases, particularly through the chords in bars 22–5 where the legato pedalling may also require practice. Marks of articulation should be taken literally (note the *portato*-style tenuto notes, enhancing the irregular rhythm) and also enjoyed: the short accented quaver in bar 8 is a gift for show-offs!

The *Hold back slightly* at the end is a wonderful opportunity to make a grand exit; the player should make much of the pause, then dash off the final quavers with panache.

C:6 Kabalevsky *Dance*

This is a cheeky dance from the twentieth-century master of children's pieces and the disguised study. The study here is of clearly articulated staccato 3rds, but the *scherzando* marking and title 'Dance' are in no way unfounded: it is in fact a characterful and jolly piece.

The 3rds are to be clear, light and short. This can be achieved by giving a bounce of the hand from a balanced arm and slightly high wrist, though much depends on the age and size of the pupil. Young, thin arms and hands may not have the weight behind the fingers to achieve a reliable and positive tone, so experiment with wrist height and speed-into/spring-out-of the key until a fluid, relaxed balance is achieved. It is not a staccato from the elbow as this is too cumbersome and would lead to some tension, particularly in the left hand from bar 24.

Once the technique for the 3rds is mastered, performing the piece is a matter of building up stamina and avoiding tension creeping in as the piece progresses. Working in gradually larger sections will pay dividends.

The essence of the piece lies in the finer control and musical detail. A brighter top to the 3rds will really help the buoyancy, as will dynamic shape across the phrases – the accents not equally loud but graded according to their position in the melody. The melody should project with authority in bars 25–31.

Throughout the whole a steady and unflappable pulse should be maintained, except perhaps in bar 38 where a slight 'easing in' of the tempo could enhance the mischievous dance.

GRADE 5

School exams often become a serious threat to practice around Grade 5, so forward planning is helpful to ease the pressure. The preparation time for this grade will need to be longer than for the previous grades, but some light pieces that are quick to absorb will help to maintain enjoyment in playing while the exam work is being systematically covered.

A:1 Mozart *Andante in B flat*

This beautiful piece by the child Mozart seems to epitomize the elegance of the eighteenth century in its unhurried grace and poise. The texture is mainly two-part, with only the occasional addition of inner right-hand notes.

The notes should not present any major difficulties, but flexibility is needed to ensure smooth use of the thumb on black keys and for the descending 6ths in bars 12 and 38. Changing fingers for successive notes in bars 2 and 3, although not obligatory, is less cumbersome than using a repeated thumb.

Neat fingerwork is needed for the figuration and, while the Andante tempo must eventually be felt in two-in-a-bar, initial practice thinking in quaver beats will ensure that all the detail is in place. Potential rhythmic hazards are the switch to demisemiquavers at bars 10 and 36 and the quavers/crotchet figure at bars 13–15, which will seem very slow after the quicker-moving notes.

There are few dynamic clues, so the pupil must use imagination and sensitivity to shape phrases towards climax points, many of which occur on the first beat of the bar. Imagining perhaps the sustained tone of an oboe or violin might help to achieve a sense of 'line' in the right hand and although many phrases consist of either one or two bars, thinking in longer units will give greater continuity and flow (bars 13–17, for example, can be regarded as one 'sentence'). Ornaments must be smoothly incorporated into the musical line, and the cadential trills at bars 16 and 42, which begin on the upper note, may contain either four or six (sextuplet) demisemiquavers.

Care should be taken to detach lightly the end of two-note slurs, but longer phrase marks (such as over the demisemiquavers in bar 10) may be regarded as bowing marks, where an audible separation at phrase endings would be inappropriate. Gently detaching the unslurred left-hand notes will give musical interest to the supporting bass part.

A:2 D. Scarlatti *Sonata in A*

Although Scarlatti is overshadowed by his two more famous contemporaries, J. S. Bach and Handel, his output of more than 500 single-movement harpsichord sonatas constitutes an important part of the keyboard repertoire. One can sense the sunny carefree atmosphere of the composer's native Italy in this binary-form sonata, one of his most delightful and outgoing in the genre.

The right hand does most of the work, so clear and incisive fingerwork, with no overlap of sounds, needs to be developed. The tempo must convey the piece's buoyant mood while being sufficiently steady to allow tonal and rhythmic definition to the semiquaver, demisemiquaver figures in bars 10–14. The change of fingers in bar 5 and similar will facilitate clarity and lightness of attack. Elsewhere fingering is often based on scalic patterns, but the final bars of each half will need special care. Trills, which should lead straight into the following semiquavers, may be fingered with 3-2 if the fourth finger proves troublesome.

A stylish performance will rely considerably on confident, authoritative phrasing. Slurring bars 15–17 and 37–9 in couplets requires flexible movement in the hand for the second note to be released clearly and gently, but elsewhere playing the semiquavers legato will probably be the most practical choice at this tempo (and grade). Buoyancy and impetus can be given to the rhythm by detaching quavers in both hands, and light upbeat notes in the right hand at bars 4, 6 and 8 will highlight the first beat of the following bar. A gentle displaced accent on the tied quaver in bar 10 and similar will help to communicate the almost jazzy rhythmic character.

Imagining a harpsichord sound will help to create a bright rather than heavy tone in *forte* passages, and much should be made of the 'echoes' in bars 12–13 and 34–5. Arpeggiating the first chord of each half to give greater presence and character is a stylish detail worth exploring.

A:3 J. N. Hummel *Scherzo in A*

Well-developed fingers are essential for this piece, which will be a good choice for pupils who enjoy the athletic side of piano playing. In addition, however, sensitive phrasing and dynamic shaping are needed to capture the charm and elegance of the music.

Examiners often hear candidates trying to play as fast as possible, especially in music with its own rhythmic momentum – sometimes with disastrous results! Although the tempo needs to be sufficiently brisk to convey a one-in-a-bar scherzo, the wise candidate will look at the piece's most difficult section – probably bars 53–60 – to find the clue to the most suitable tempo. Fingering of semiquavers, which are often based on scale patterns, must be sorted out (and adhered to) at the outset of study. Slow practice will help to ensure that co-ordination between hands is secure and that patterns are committed to the finger memory. Evenness of tone must be aimed for at the position changes in bars 37–40, and care taken not to slow down when leaping upwards with both hands at bars 56–7.

A wide dynamic range is needed to convey the music's character, and quieter levels require especial control. Practising scales at different tonal levels, including crescendo and diminuendo, listening for evenness of rhythm and tone, might prove beneficial.

A light, flexible wrist and arm will ensure a graceful unaccented final note to the three-note melodic figure that pervades the piece. Balancing of the accompaniment, which is usually in the left hand, requires the pupil to listen carefully, and light second and third beats will ensure rhythmic buoyancy.

A small hand may not be able to create long legato lines in the left hand at bar 61 onwards, so phrasing in couplets (as in bars 70–71) is a suitable alternative. An effective ending will be created by playing as quietly as possible, slowing down or not according to choice.

A:4 J. S. Bach *(Little) Prelude No. 4 in A minor*

Pupils often choose the shortest pieces, presuming them to be an easy option! However, this seventeen-bar Prelude, which with its rich contrapuntal interest is in the style of a two-part Invention, contains some potential pitfalls. It should therefore be selected by candidates with good independence between the hands and the patience to learn the notes reliably. Listening to a harpsichord will draw the player into the Baroque sound-world.

Separate-hands practice is needed to establish the note-patterns and, as importantly, the fingering. Some unusual twists of tonality occur at certain points, so accidentals should be carefully checked, especially those that recur in a bar (e.g. the right hand's F# in bar 7).

Exploring the contrapuntal writing with its imitation between the hands (in bars 3–4 the left hand copies in the dominant key the right hand of bars 1–2) will make sense of the texture. Some pupils may like to imagine the lines played by instruments, violin and cello for example. As the focus of musical interest switches between the hands, the pupil must develop skill in balancing the tone for the appropriate contrapuntal lines to be highlighted. Practising scales, with alternating dynamic levels between the hands, listening carefully for clarity, will help to achieve this.

Before working on phrasing, most players like to master the intricacies of hands together. In bars 4 and 5 care should be taken to co-ordinate the detail; also needing attention are bars 9 and 14. If done smoothly, dividing the notes between the hands in bar 16 will work well.

Playing all quavers staccato is perhaps the simplest phrasing option, but slurring adjacent notes while detaching leaps provides a more interesting and stylish effect. Rests in the left hand should be clearly observed, and clean articulation is needed for the semiquavers. The tempo in performance should reflect the compound time signature with its three main beats, yet not be so fast as to lose control and with it the detail.

A:5 F. X. Dušek *Presto*

Candidates who enjoy bright, cheerful music will be attracted to this sonata movement by Dušek, an underrated contemporary of Haydn. Although the piece extends for three pages, the beginning of the final section (from bar 70) of the sonata-form structure is identical to the opening eight bars, thus helping the learning process. Notes are relatively straightforward and the piece presents few intricacies; there is however need for a reliable sense of pulse and for fluency at a brisk tempo.

The suggested metronome mark of crotchet = 120 will give a sense of momentum without being too fast for clarity. Changing from quavers to semiquavers and vice versa needs care to avoid distortion of the basic pulse, and ritardandos must be incorporated subtly, before returning immediately to tempo.

Short, incisive staccato in both hands will give rhythmic vitality and contrast to the legato phrasing. The suggested pedalling helps to highlight certain important points, but you may wish to modify it at bars 29 and 31, for example, to allow the rests to register.

Confident projection of the dynamic detail (rarely well done on an unfamiliar piano) breathes life into the phrasing. The shape of each section will be helped by thinking in long units, especially at the start of the development at bar 35 where each figure is only one bar long. Listening to music from the Classical period played on historic instruments will assist in creating the appropriate sound quality – the *fortes* bright rather than heavy.

The musical interest is usually carried by the right hand, so careful listening is needed to judge the level of sound for the accompaniment. The staccato-chord passage at bars 25–8, however, suggests equal importance for both hands.

A few appropriate adjectives – bright, happy, surprising – written on the score may help to create the right spirit in performance, for clear and quick-witted characterization is the key to gaining a good mark for this piece.

A:6 Handel *Toccata in G minor*

A toccata (from *toccare*, to touch) is usually a lively piece that shows off a player's dexterity and control. This beautiful movement will suit a pupil with a reliable sense of pulse and also the patience and organization needed to negotiate the numerous ornaments.

Although it must convey four, not eight, beats in a bar, the tempo chosen will be dictated largely by the ornaments and phrasing detail. The bass part, which provides a stable foundation for the florid right hand, should be practised separately, perhaps imagining a cello or bassoon providing the mixture of slurred and detached quavers.

Some initial hands-together practice without ornaments is always useful for establishing a rhythmic framework; this will prevent disruption of the basic pulse once ornamentation is included. Performance directions are clearly set out, with most of the ornament realizations feasible at this grade (two demisemiquavers followed by one semiquaver may be the better option at bar 8, however). A few editorial notes in smaller print, for example in bar 5, should be incorporated if possible.

The piece was written originally for harpsichord, an instrument on which successful characterization comes largely from clarity of phrasing; the editorial suggestions help to achieve this by providing a variety of ways to articulate the quavers and semiquavers, highlighting certain important notes within each group. Practising scales or exercises staccato will help to develop the necessary hand and finger flexibility for detaching unslurred notes clearly.

All dynamic decisions are left to the performer, giving free rein to a graceful shaping of the melodic lines. Useful stylistic starting-points are the places where the dynamic levels may be 'terraced' (e.g. bars 3–4), or where there are echo effects, such as in bars 13–14 (and in bar 13, fourth beat, the pupil must remember to repeat the C♯ in the left hand). Correct for this style is a bright *forte* tone, and a full, interesting dynamic range will only emerge if the *pianos* are sufficiently quiet.

B:1 J. F. F. Burgmüller *La chevaleresque*

A knight in search of adventure? Maybe, but this knight seems rather timid, only gaining in courage as the end of his escapade approaches! Nevertheless, a sturdy, march-like pace, certainly no faster than crotchet = *c.*126, is required – and the final choice of tempo may, in part, be dictated by the semiquaver runs near the end. The opening pulse can be established by the wrist and forearm motion: after a short light attack on the first chord, a firm set of fingertips will be lifted out of the keys in an uninhibited (but not exaggerated) trajectory before landing on the next chord, and so on. This will aid the music's rhythmic character. To this end it is also important, in places such as bars 2 and 4, to keep the right-hand semiquavers short and snappy.

In contrast, bars 17–24 need a real legato in both hands, the left-hand Cs being held down for as long as possible. Although the application of pedal is not necessary elsewhere, pedalling by the half-bar in this section will complement the textural change.

The dynamics are surprisingly restrained for much of the time, although eventually some strong, bold tone is required; this can be produced by a relaxed but controlled forearm drop. Dynamic shading is indicated in several places and you might consider commencing the runs in bars 9 and 11 at a *mezzo-forte* level, to allow for the marked crescendo. The type of crescendo/diminuendo effect called for in bars 19 and 20 can be incorporated into scale practice: try increasing and decreasing the tone of a chromatic scale to and from the middle of an ascending and descending octave, but within the overall context of *piano*.

Fun can be had imagining what exactly the knight is getting up to; whatever this is, however, it never seems to change his musical pace.

B:2 Reger *Gigue*

This lively, really rather dramatic gigue needs plenty of momentum and contrast, underpinned by a stable two-in-a-bar feel. The tempo of dotted crotchet = *c*.108 works well, although a more confident player could increase this to *c*.116 without the risk of rushing.

There are a number of technical features requiring practice, the first of which involves the two hands in contrasting staccato and slurred articulations, such as those found in bars 4–8. Beware of too much separate-hands practice here; it is the sensation of co-ordinated difference that your pupil really needs to assimilate. The staccato notes call for a real finger staccato from a firm tip and rounded first joint.

The hand arrangements suggested in brackets at bars 14 and 16 are clearly optimal. But in 16 larger hands can finger the left-hand chord 2/4/5, and the right-hand chord with 4 on D♭, leaving 5 for the subsequent E♭. There is no easy solution to executing the jumps between the hand positions in the right hand of bars 18–21, but keeping the hand well in and away from the edges of the keys will help to minimize the degree of awkwardness involved. The final three notes of the piece can comfortably be fingered 3-2-1, if your pupil would prefer not to risk leaping!

There are no long phrases to consider, but careful observance of the slurred couplets in bars 9, 35 and 36 will project the rhythmic play of the hemiolas that result. The dynamics cover a big range from *pianissimo* to *fortissimo*, and the opening can be quite explosive: forceful but not ugly. Although the markings are polarized, favouring either *forte*/*fortissimo* or *piano*/*pianissimo*, there is clearly some rise and fall within the extremes.

The best performances of this piece should fill the exam room with a blaze of sound and activity. The music will no doubt appeal to the extroverts among your pupils.

B:3 Reinecke *Romance*

This song-like piece will be attractive to the daydreaming temperament and, while it makes no demands on your pupil's agility, it does require a refined sense of balance.

Much of the piece adopts a three-part texture, the upper voice of which should be projected the most strongly. The bass notes can then underpin the melodic line with a supporting, if background, firmness, while the middle part needs the least emphasis. It may be useful to practise just top and bottom parts, making careful judgements concerning the balance, and getting used to the harmonic outlines and related phrase shapes. The middle part may also be practised on its own to cultivate a smooth transfer of notes between the hands; it can then be reintroduced gently into the texture. The half-bar pedalling indicated will bring out the music's textural quality, and may continue to be employed effectively in places such as bars 4 and 8.

The touch used to project the upper voice needs to be deep, firm and super-legato but also able to sculpt the phrases, easing off at the ends of phrases and avoiding any emphasis on such notes as the Fs in bars 3 and 7. Much of the dynamic shading operates between levels of *piano* and *mezzo-forte*, and even the *forte* in bar 17 is full rather than forceful. Use of the *una corda* pedal will enhance the sound quality of the *pianissimo* moments. The chords in the very last bar may be played with a light staccato touch, the sound cushioned by direct pedalling.

Discreet application of rubato can heighten the expressive character of the turns in bars 6 and 28, highlight the key change at bars 39–40 – and help to delineate the phrases. It is an idea for someone to sing the melody while your pupil provides the accompaniment, as understanding breathing can be most instructive where phrasing is concerned.

B:4 Massenet *Mélodie*

Marked *con malinconia* (with melancholy), this piece is a real 'weepy' and is definitely one for the romantics among your pupils.

Perhaps issues concerning balance and texture pose the biggest challenges to both technique and imagination. All staccato notes occur within phrase marks and playing these notes with a dry, clipped staccato is liable to reduce the piece to a travesty of its true self. Where staccato is marked, a detached touch – firm in the left hand, light in the right – is desirable, but this should be tempered by pedal use. Changes on the bar and half-bar will work in places such as bars 1–4, but elsewhere (e.g. bar 14) pedalling may need to match the quaver movement. Do not worry that the left-hand demisemiquaver rests will be hidden by the pedal sonority – the rest can be reflected by a subtle delay to the sounded demisemiquaver E.

The right-hand quavers should throb gently, like heartbeats, but must not intrude because almost all the melodic interest lies in the left hand. Generally, the left wrist should be raised a little higher above the keyboard than the right so that the touch can be deep. The right hand may be kept close to the keyboard, engaged only in small movements.

Always think in phrases rather than in beats. Some phrases are in four-bar units, such as that spanning the second quaver of bar 1 to the first quaver of bar 5. Others are in two-bar units, an example of which runs from the second quaver of bar 10 to the first of bar 12. The tendency for the phrases to 'droop' can be reflected in the dynamics, although in bars 10–15 a mounting intensity may be felt, which eases off as bar 17 is approached.

If you know any good cellists, do get one to play the left-hand part; in this way, much can be learnt about cantabile – and *malinconia*.

B:5 Nielsen *Doll's March*

Many intriguing images are suggested by this understated march, one of which could depict a small automaton moving along in a mechanistically inhuman manner!

A tempo of crotchet = *c.*126 yields a suitable tempo, although the nimble-fingered may increase this to *c.*132. But whatever tempo is adopted, it is important that it is retained, because no rubato is required and stability of pulse is essential to the music's integrity.

The left-hand semiquavers in bar 8 may be executed comfortably if fingered 1-2-3-1-2-3, as long as the first thumb does not create an accent. In bar 17, the right-hand fourth finger can be passed over the fifth (as smoothly as possible) to avoid breaking the melodic line, and a raising of the forearm will enable the slight emphasis needed on the G. In bar 21, however, a large hand can achieve a similar effect by playing the B♭ with the fourth finger and the C with the fifth. Clarity of articulation on the final B♭s in bar 35 may be aided by splitting the three notes between the hands in a left-right-left arrangement or, possibly, by taking the last two B♭s with the right hand, fingering 3-2.

Generally, a light touch is desirable throughout, employing as needed a precise, crisp staccato executed from the fingertip. The right-hand accents need to be highlighted but this should be in context: the accents are rhythmic pointers and not sledgehammers! A careful calculation of the exact weighting needed will, when put into practice, greatly add to the piece's character. The predominant dynamic is *piano* and even the *forte* needs some care, because sound in the treble register can all too easily turn harsh if produced over-forcefully. The *una corda* pedal may helpfully be employed in the last two bars.

Examiners will enjoy performances that not only demonstrate rhythmic discipline but also bring out the quirky humour of the music.

B:6 Schumann *Waltz*

This Romantic dance has little of the glamour of the typical Strauss waltz, and is instead infused with a passionate *Ernst*. The outer parts demand a sense of commitment and tonal weight (though never brute force), while a brighter, less intense manner is suggested by the central section (bars 17–28) in which a lighter touch will complement the music's major modality.

The wide leaps in the left hand may present a technical challenge; a good preparatory drill involves isolating each leap from the context of the piece, firstly playing the lower note and then moving rapidly rightwards along the keyboard. Once the hand is over the upper chord, it should be kept poised there for a split second or two, fingers accurately aligned, before dropping into the keys. By gradually speeding up this process, an appropriate kinaesthetic sensation is developed through which accuracy tends to become habitual.

A tempo of crotchet = *c.*160 works well, but a one-in-the-bar feeling should be encouraged. Use of rubato around bars 19–20 and 27–8 can enhance the left hand's melodic contour. The *sforzando* markings in the left hand at bars 8 and 36, and the right-hand accents in bars 12 and 40, need some highlighting but this can be achieved by a hair's-breadth delay as well as by a slight dynamic emphasis. The ending needs to be strong although containing, perhaps, no more than a hint of a ritenuto.

The score instructs *Mit Pedal* and the music's textures will benefit from this help. Pedal changes on the first beat of each bar will work but, to avoid blurring, extra changes may be needed at places such as bars 8 and 15, to match the changing harmony. If the left-hand 10ths in bars 16 and 44 need to be split, the pedal change must catch the low A to ensure harmonic sense.

This piece is ideal for those pupils whose temperament and fingers respond to Romantic harmony and who have a good sense of voicing and colour.

C:1 Martha Mier *Jackson Street Blues*

The relaxed swing and tunefulness of *Jackson Street Blues* are sure to prove popular with teenagers. You can almost hear the honky-tonk piano and the Southern drawl of the blues singer as you play. After a two-bar introduction a soulful melody begins, and throughout the piece there is an interplay between 'vocals' and accompaniment which is not hard to identify.

Since the accompaniment moves across quite a large span of notes, it would be worthwhile establishing a really confident left hand before trying to play hands together. It will soon be noticed that there are regular chord sequences, which are sometimes the same but sometimes slightly altered. Adding pedal enriches the sonority of the chords and makes it easier to move freely across the keyboard. The pedal should be used almost continuously, changing with the harmony, but leaving a space for the staccato chord in bar 2 (and similar). If the regular pedal-changing stops in bar 4 to give clarity to the low bass notes, it needs to resume just after – not on or before – the first beat of the next bar to prevent a smudge.

Pairs of quavers should be swung so that they sound in a crotchet/ quaver rhythm throughout the piece, even if the first quaver is represented by a rest (as in bars 11 and 12). Once established, the swinging will feel quite natural, creating the 'easy relaxed tempo' that the composer describes. The player should be alert for the changes of accidentals within a bar, but also notice where they remain the same. In bar 3, for instance, the last right-hand quaver will still be D♯ even though the chord underneath has a D♮.

The composer has provided ample dynamic marks, and if these are followed and the melody sings warmly, your pupil is well on the way to an expressive performance.

C:2 Windsperger *Burlesque*

A burlesque is a parody or comic scenario. In this piece one could imagine the wind snatching somebody's hat and tossing it about as the unfortunate person tries to catch it again. Or perhaps it depicts the antics of clowns? Whatever is decided, the gusty dynamics, rushing semiquavers and sudden changes of tempo create a boisterous and amusing picture.

Beginning this piece too fast will be a recipe for disaster, because the stringendo (hurrying) at bar 5 continues until bar 13. Here, at the climax of the scene, the beat should become constant, allowing the cross-rhythms to create their own excitement.

Both hands will need some independent practice, because co-ordination could be a problem. Later, when putting the hands together, slow practice will help to ensure accuracy and control, especially in bars 13–20. However, while slow practice is always useful, it does not provide all the answers. When the piece is hands-together and safely in the fingers, some beat-to-beat practice could help to develop pace in a secure way. For instance, the notes of just a beat or two could be played at speed, always beginning and ending on the first note of a beat; when this feels comfortable, more and more beats can be safely joined together.

If the right hand's fingering in the opening phrase does not suit, the thumb could go instead on the E, and 4-3-2 used on the repeated A♭ quavers. This will then match what appears in bar 3, and such finger sequences are often more secure and easier to learn. The acciaccaturas in bar 5 may prove troublesome because the hands move in the same direction, so the player should begin by striking both notes together in each hand, and once this feels easy, a quick flick of the fingers will produce a really crisp effect.

On account of its quirky, knockabout character, this is an excellent choice for the performer who enjoys witty and colourful music.

C:3 Dejan Despić *Fanfare*

Imagine the brilliant sound of brass instruments as this impressive *Fanfare* is played. It falls into three clearly defined sections. Firstly, three trumpets announce the theme with its distinctive rising 4ths, and eleven bars later this is boldly answered by the trombones. The third section begins with the same rising-4th motif (bar 16), but now it starts to fade, and the fanfare dies away into the distance.

Confusion could arise over which notes are held and which are detached or staccato, especially where the parts overlap. As it is a piece that could be practised hands-together almost at once, learning just a few bars at a time could be a help, taking care to play exactly what is written. The *sempre non legato* at the beginning refers to all the quavers and most of the crotchets. Longer notes and, of course, tied notes should be sustained.

It will be important to play strictly in time so that the changes of metre and different bar-lengths can make their full impact. At bar 10 (and bars 15–16), the three accented chords should be marked firmly, and the quaver chords played with a crisp staccato. This will provide space for the last note in the bar, which is the upbeat quaver of the new phrase. In the last section, the rests must be counted carefully for rushing to be avoided, and it will be better to think of the *smorzando* (dying away) as referring more to the dynamics than to the tempo. A slight relaxing of the speed will feel natural, but it should not be allowed to undermine the rhythmic patterns of the last few bars.

As more than half of the piece is *forte* or louder, care must be taken to produce a good quality of sound. Any hint of tension will result in harshness, so encourage supple wrists and the use of arm weight to produce a big tone.

C:4 Mike Cornick *Espagnol*

In recent years the List C pieces have included some gems, and this melancholy Spanish piece is one of them. It presents little technical difficulty so long as your pupil uses the pedal reliably, has a secure sense of rhythm and can produce a warm cantabile tone.

There is only one main theme, which is repeated with subtle variations in notes and rhythm; it is important that these differences are noticed in the early stages of learning. Initially it will be useful to be able to switch from counting four crotchets to two minims in a bar so as to make certain that the beat is not disturbed by the rhythmic inflections and flowing triplets. If necessary a metronome, set at about minim = 40, may be used to pace the counting, but its use should be limited. Alterations to the rhythm often occur at or just before the cadences, and as the composer has asked for even quavers (not swung), the differences between quavers, semiquavers and triplets should be heard. Once the piece is flowing accurately, the player can relax a little and just feel a slow two-in-a-bar – this will better express the mood of nostalgia and *mañana.*

Because of the level of repetition, it will be essential to make the most of dynamic contrasts and to highlight different treatments of the repeated material, especially any changes in harmony. In the last four bars, for example, there is a descending chromatic bass line, which is set against 3rds in the right hand.

Time should be taken over the last two bars, holding the melody note D above the spread chord for the dissonance to be emphasized, and delaying the final bass note so that the richness of its sonority, quiet though it is, can be relished.

C:5 Gillock *Mister Trumpet Man*

It is always a good idea to have a piece in your repertoire that allows you to let off steam! *Mister Trumpet Man* is just such a piece, and great fun too. It needs a sturdy attack and a strong sense of swing, so is definitely not for the faint-hearted.

There are quite a few jumps to negotiate and – with the relentless beat driving the music along – there is no time to think twice over where to land.

A first step, therefore, would be to look at the groups of chords and play them so that the hands get used to the shape and position of each one. Your pupil will quickly discover that there are only a few different chords and that they are all situated in the same part of the keyboard. The three main chords are versions of I, IV and V with jazzy added 6ths, 7ths and 9ths. A few versions of chord ii, with added 7th, and occasional chromatic alteration, complete the harmonic palette.

While the notes and rhythm are being learnt in lessons, this piece could easily be played as a duet for pupil and teacher, one taking all the chords and the other the melody.

The mixed notation should not deter your pupil. The predominant feel is swing, that is triplets or 'swung quavers'. Wherever the dotted-quaver, semiquaver pattern occurs, it will sound convincing to continue swinging just as though the pattern were triplet crotchet–quaver figures.

The player should make the most of those bars that are *piano* or *mezzo-piano* so that there is plenty of dynamic interest, but accents need to be marked firmly, especially those occurring on syncopated notes or at ends of phrases. Pedal is really only required where marked, since a spiky, rather dry effect sounds right for this style.

Mister Trumpet Man is full of good humour and raw energy, and will be enjoyed by many.

C:6 Gabriel Jackson *October Monody*

Monody was the name given to a solo song of lamentation in Greek tragedy (from the Greek word *monoideia*). Much later, in the early 1600s, it became popular as a recitative-like melody for voice with accompaniment. Gabriel Jackson's own words – '... my pieces are made of simple melodies, chords, drones and ostinatos' – help to put *October Monody* in perspective.

At first glance this piece may seem to be a very easy option in view of the limited number of notes that the composer uses. Apart from the final chord, the left hand has only one interval (a 4th) to play as accompaniment, and the single-line melody roams around within a nine-note range. However, its very simplicity, reminiscent of some of Stravinsky's melodies, and the detail in the articulation make it more of a challenge.

As a starting-point it would be useful to look at the phrase structure. The composer employs the technique of increasing phrase-lengths, with the first phrase five bars, the second phrase seven bars and the third phrase ten bars long. The song is completed by an almost identical repeat of the first phrase but with its third bar omitted and two extra bars tacked on, making it six bars in length. By understanding this structure it becomes easier to give shape to the piece and to develop an understanding of what the music is saying.

'Pedalling is at the performer's discretion', we are told, and – if applied sensitively and changed at fairly regular intervals – pedal does help to give the thin texture greater sonority. However, every stressed note and slur should be clearly marked, and when practising the right hand alone, the declamatory nature of the tune should be kept in mind. Dynamics and intensity increase as the phrases lengthen, and the climax is reached in the third phrase where the highest notes are found. With all passion spent, the last phrase is played quietly except for the unexpected final chord.

GRADE 6

The big hurdle of Grade 5 Theory, Practical Musicianship or Grade 5 Jazz will be successfully over as work begins on Grade 6. The slightly different criteria for the higher grades, printed in *These Music Exams,* emphasize the need for the musical character, style and details to come across with conviction. Hopefully, by now the technical fluency will support these developing ideas, allowing more focus on expressive stylistic aspects.

A:1 Beethoven *Larghetto maestoso–Allegro assai*

The 'Appassionata' Sonata, that landmark of the repertoire, was written some twenty years later than this youthful work, yet even here the thirteen-year-old composer was exploring the dramatic possibilities of F minor.

The powerful opening section sounds orchestral in character, and if the apparent extremes of dynamics are considered in terms of *forte* representing the full orchestra and *piano* just small groups of instruments, they can more easily be contained within a musical framework. The repeated quavers in bars 11–12 should be thought of as drumbeats underpinning the chords rising above, and when the hands play in unison, the player must listen carefully to achieve good co-ordination. He or she might imagine being the conductor controlling different instruments in the orchestra.

Pedal will help to support the tone in several places (the Larghetto's minim chords, for instance, and the tremolando figures in bars 31–4), but care should be taken not to smudge harmony changes or obscure articulation details. If the left-hand fingering in bars 5–7 seems complicated, keep the thumb on the repeated note (the F in bar 5), simply reaching over to the higher note with the second finger. All semiquaver figures require agile fingers, especially in bars 28–9 where the mixture of slurs and staccato will need extra practice.

The function of the trills in bars 16–17 is merely to create accents on the semiquaver groups, so if necessary an acciaccatura will suffice (and is less likely to disturb the beat). The other potentially problematic trills are the five-note turns suggested in bars 18–19. Once fingering is decided, time needs to be devoted just to this right-hand passage, ensuring that one crotchet joins smoothly to the next.

In the brief development section, a new idea emerges at bar 41. Attention must be paid to the balance here, as the left hand could easily overwhelm the melody. The moving notes of the Alberti figure can come across, but keep the repeated F comparatively quiet.

Despite the mood of urgency in the fast sections, your pupil must keep a firm grip on the pulse. Any running away will not only weaken the music's dramatic strength but may also lead to technical downfall.

This single movement provides an excellent introduction to the wonderful world of Beethoven's piano sonatas.

A:2 Handel *Gigue*

The gigue is a lively dance often used as the rousing finale to a suite. Like all dances of its kind, this beautiful example by Handel will require agile fingers and crisp articulation to bring out the brightness and buoyancy of its texture. This could be achieved by playing all the quavers staccato, but greater musical interest can be achieved by slurring a few chosen ones.

Given that early keyboard players used the slur for expressive purposes or as a type of accent, notes that seem more important or create a dissonance could be slurred. For example, you could slur the first two quavers of the second beat of bar 1, then the first two quavers of the first beat of bar 2. As the left hand follows in imitation, the same slurring should appear there too. Indeed, the slurs will make this canonic feature more audible. In bars 3 and 4 a slur on the first two quavers of the second beat will highlight the dissonances that occur. There are, of course, other ways of slurring the piece, but whichever notes you decide to slur, it is then a question of finding similar patterns throughout the dance.

When the texture becomes three- or four-part, there emerge longer notes which need to be sustained in order to fill out the harmony. This textural thickening is often used to add weight to important cadences, such as bars 8, 12, 14, 16, and 23; if slurs are used on both first and second beats of these bars, it will not only emphasize the chords but make them easier to play.

As with any contrapuntal music, taking out individual 'voices' and rehearsing them alone will be time well spent. This way one becomes more aware of the special features of the music. Dynamics are, as usual, left to the performer, but it is worth remembering that lively pieces usually began *forte.* The way in which phrases ascend or descend in pitch, and the different colours of keys, can also suggest changes in dynamics. Pupils should be encouraged to make their own decisions and to take an active interest in this important aspect of musical interpretation.

A:3 Casanovas *Sonata in F*

The carefree mood and simplicity of notes and texture will make this sonata by the Spanish composer Casanovas a popular choice. With almost no large chords and only a few light octaves in the left hand, it is ideal for the pupil with smaller hands. The style and form owes more to the composer's famous compatriot of an earlier age, Domenico Scarlatti, than it does to Casanovas's contemporaries elsewhere in Europe.

The only tricky features are the timing and articulation of the groups of quick notes, which are actually written-out ornaments. In bar 1 there is the turn and in bar 15 the inverted turn followed by the slide; bars 26 and 28 present two forms of the short trill. These five ornaments should be practised meticulously in time while counting out loud or tapping the beat (a metronome could be used instead). In bars 15 and 17 it should be remembered that the triplet group and slide are worth only half a quaver beat each. Once the ornaments are flowing comfortably, the left hand can be added. Initially it is an idea to practise at a slower tempo until the ear and fingers become accustomed to the co-ordination of both parts.

Alberti-style figuration will need individual practice in order to become correctly balanced. The repeated notes are invariably played by the thumb (for example, bars 13–18 in the left hand, and bars 19–22 in the right); it is important to keep the hand balanced so that the thumb remains light with just enough weight being directed to the fingers carrying the melodic notes. This is especially necessary in the passage beginning in bar 25 where the descending left-hand notes form a counter-melody to the right-hand tune. A light, controlled arm rotation can facilitate the playing of these figures, especially when the intervals widen out towards an octave.

The few dynamic marks should be regarded as a guide to the general level of a given passage. 'Echo' dynamics could add colour in repeated phrases, and rising and falling figures afford the possibility for crescendo and diminuendo. A reliable fingering in the last few bars will enable the piece to end brilliantly with a flourish.

A:4 J. S. Bach *Allemande*

The French Suites of J. S. Bach are often the pianist's first introduction to the Baroque suite. They are technically less demanding than the English Suites or Partitas, and contain some lovely music. Each suite opens with an allemande, a moderately paced dance of German origin, usually serious in character, which begins with a single upbeat semiquaver or group of three. A suitable metronome speed for this allemande is crotchet = *c*.52.

The texture of the piece is almost entirely two-part; it becomes four-part only in the final bar of each section. This does not mean, however, that the piece is especially easy. Imitation, phrasing and ornamentation must all be carefully managed.

Editions vary as to what embellishments to play. In the Associated Board's edition, the compound ornament of appoggiatura + mordent (see bar 1 and similar) could prove to be a stumbling block. Played well, it creates a very lovely effect, but the simple mordent that appears in many of the other editions may be an easier option.

The most effective articulation here is to play semiquavers usually legato and most of the quavers lightly detached. However, a few strategically placed dots and slurs will make the phrasing more expressive, giving 'lift' and character (especially where there is a sequence). In the right hand, the quavers before the tied notes in bars 1 and 3 could be detached to give an extra 'pointing' or weight to the syncopation; and slurs could be placed on the first two semiquavers of the third and fourth beats in bars 2 and 3 (and similar situations).

Dynamics should not be too extreme in this gently flowing dance, but they should respond to the rise and fall of the phrasing and the mood of the harmony. The player must watch out for the changes from minor to major, and give due attention to the interrupted cadence in bar 22 – an important climax.

A:5 Bečvařovský *Polonaise*

It is interesting to find a polonaise set out with such precisely marked accents and pedalling. If all the details are faithfully followed and a firm pulse is maintained, the special rhythmic characteristics of the polonaise are bound to come alive. The piece may therefore serve as a guide to performing other examples of the dance.

The direction *Maestoso e nobile* reflects the majestic character of this processional dance, and a tempo of crotchet = 84–8 will allow time for the placing of accents, and space for the written-out turns in, for example, bar 12.

The less usual pedal marks (*P* for depressing the pedal, and x to release) might lead the eye to read *P* instead as a dynamic mark; the player will however soon get used to them. The results are effective, especially in highlighting the second-beat accent at the main cadences, negotiating the leaps in the middle section and in adding tone and brilliance generally.

The trill in bar 29 (and 30) should begin on the principal note. Initially think of it as a semiquaver triplet (DED) plus four demisemiquavers (EDCD) so that it fits with the left hand. Later, up to speed, it will sound like a septuplet flowing to the next beat. In the coda, the turn will require a triplet demisemiquaver group on the second semiquaver of the (first) beat. End the turn with the thumb so that the step up to the A♯ is comfortable.

There is a change of mood for the Trio (marked *con grazia*). The melody is more lyrical for a few bars and here it is worth remembering that the polonaise displays two very conflicting images – love and war. The left hand, entrusted with the accompaniment, must give rhythmic support but remain quieter than the melody throughout. Too often candidates will play both hands equally strongly during crescendos and in *forte* passages, so encourage them to gently increase arm weight on the fingers that play the melody, as the crescendo is made. The repeated chords are usually staccato (even when pedal is used) but the 'rocking' figures (first heard at bar 5) should be played more legato.

For exam purposes the repeats (together with the first-time bars) will have to be omitted, but the da capo should be played. Then, second time around, the eye will need to get used to moving quickly from the *Fine* bar to the coda, so as not to delay the final grand flourish.

A:6 B. Marcello *Presto*

Vitality and good humour abound in this delightful Presto by the Italian Benedetto Marcello. As is usual in Baroque keyboard music, agile finger-work is essential, and the texture must be transparent and balanced at all times. The student should be especially careful over semiquaver figures where there are repeated notes. In bars 5–8, for instance, the repeated D must be kept quieter than the other notes for a melody line to emerge.

Although much of this piece falls into two-bar phrases, there are occasions where convincing four-bar phrases can be produced – with the careful use of dynamics or merely a sense of forward propulsion. The first four bars are a good example. The music rises to the middle and falls to a suspension at the perfect cadence in bar 4; by employing a crescendo and diminuendo, therefore, the four bars can be heard as one phrase. Then at bar 11 another four-bar phrase is immediately repeated an octave lower. By keeping the music moving (without hurrying, of course) and by employing the 'echo' dynamic as marked for the repeat, these bars will also flow more musically.

The suggested dynamics and articulation work well and help to project the high spirits of the music. Examiners will, however, accept alternative dynamics and articulation, so long as they are appropriate to the style. The given fingering is also helpful, but the player might consider a change for the 3rds in bars 24, 26 and 28. The traditional pattern of 3/2, 4/1, 5/3 and back again, keeping the thumb in position throughout, fits all three bars – which is an added bonus.

B:1 S. Heller *Prelude in C sharp minor*

Heller's metronome mark of crotchet = 138 for this Prelude reflects his reputation as a pianist of some merit. However, the more moderate editorial tempo mark (or less) will allow far greater character, and control, on a modern instrument.

This attractive, charming piece sounds technically easy, yet much work is needed to achieve this apparent simplicity. The semiquaver patterns require working into the finger memory, so consistent fingering is a must. Giving musical shape to the phrases will prevent the piece sounding like a study.

Musically the performance will rely on a persuasive charm, a small amount of rubato, delicate shaping of the melodic line and, above all, a subtlety of balance between the hands. Overly weighty chords must be avoided. The left hand's most important note of the first bar is the bottom C♯, and the following three-note chord must be considerably lighter.

Depending upon tempo and size of hand, the pedal changes up to bar 48 will be either each beat or each bar and across the bar-line (legato pedal from bass note to bass note). For bars 17–19 and 21–3 the pedal should sustain the top melodic notes and change with the harmony on every beat. Dropping onto and holding the top notes will give the desired tone here. From the end of bar 42 the pedal will need to catch and support the bass note even when the left-hand chord is spread; if the stretch allows, the finger should hold onto the note. In bars 46–7 the pedal changes are again on each beat.

Some passages need extra attention. The quick left-hand jumps in bars 7 and 15 will be easier if done without having to look at the hand. Also, bars 40–47 may require separate practice – and here, add the pedal to the left hand before hands are put together.

Subtleties of notation should be interpreted within their context. The 'hat' accents and *sforzando* are no more than arrival points, and the right hand's couplet phrasing in bars 17–19 implies only a lightening of the chord.

Dynamics should be slightly understated to avoid any boisterousness except, perhaps, from bar 40, and the end is calm and peaceful.

B:2 Schubert *Moment musical in F minor*

This popular and characterful miniature is notorious for just one bar, bar 9, where many a performance comes unstuck; bar 25 is also tricky. This apart, the piece has few technical concerns beyond confident execution of the left-hand jumps.

Crotchet = *c*.88, the suggested tempo, allows both the necessary buoyancy and plenty of time to play the trickier bars with ease. The opening left-hand figure should have character, with an energetic bottom note followed by much lighter chords. The first two bars could be a little more robust. Between bars 19 and 26 the leaps are larger and less predictable. Make quick jumps from the lower note to the top chords using the second finger as a guide, then vice versa, measuring the distance with the fifth finger. Working with eyes closed is helpful, as is encouraging the hand to travel ahead of time to prepare the notes.

To convey the dance character, the right hand's articulation and phrasing are clearly important throughout, but initial focus should be on bar 9. Starting with just the upper notes, condition the fingering into the hands while maintaining a relaxed arm. Then add the other notes, releasing the quavers as soon as they are played in order to match the left-hand articulation and help play the intermediate semiquavers.

The approach to bar 9 causes some of the problem, with hands and arms tensing in anticipation. If this happens, play up to the end of bar 8, wait, release any tension, then play on into the next two bars slowly. If this is done often, the mind will be less keen to anticipate any problem here.

As to bar 25, a 5-2 fingering on the C and E♭ chord will be quite a stretch for many. An alternative is 5-1, but pupils may have to work at the resulting thumb jumps.

Once the hands are secure separately they should slot together slowly but surely. Avoid looking much at the left hand, instead allowing it to travel instinctively to its notes. Some work with the left hand louder than the right can pay dividends.

Since much of the piece is repeated, exploring a vividly contrasting dynamic range will really boost the performance – and enjoying some playfulness with the tempo will help to capture the Russian dance character.

B:3 Suk *Melodie*

Originally for two violins, this piece is throughout a melody, or duet, with accompaniment. It will rely for its expressiveness on a sensitivity to balance as well as an instinctive rhythmic pliancy and dynamic shading. It does not always fall easily under the fingers, so extra time might be needed in preparing the work.

A successful performance will come from control of the left hand and subtle pedalling; delicacy of touch is also essential. The staccato markings imply a gentle yet detached left hand, encouraging a lightness of touch. The left hand can, however, feel quite uncertain when detached, so some work without pedal but as legato as possible will help the physical memory in the learning stages. The pedalled accompaniment sounds quite different when the left hand is played more legato, a colour saved for the warmer middle section.

As harmonic support from the held notes is important, crotchets and minims should be held with the fingers to enable small changes of pedal if necessary, particularly in bar 15. Practising the left hand and pedal together will reap rewards when hands are put together.

Pedalling needs to be flexible, as the markings are a guide only and much will depend on the instrument. Avoid relying too much on the pedal, therefore, and put a greater emphasis on holding notes with the fingers.

The one crucial element of the piece is the balance between the hands. It is through the longer melodic notes that the ears must be at their most acute – staying fixed on the decaying A in bars 1 and 2, for instance, hearing whether the left hand is becoming too dominant as the A fades and adjusting accordingly. Just as important is balance within the hand, so careful preparation will be needed in bars 7–8 and 17–18 (and similar) to maintain a sense of line.

Observing the expressive markings will help create a musical performance – as will an instinctive rubato. Dynamics need good judgement and consideration. If the many *pianissimos* are too apologetic, the melody will not project and good balance between the hands is almost impossible. There is also the *pianissississimo* at the end to consider.

In the final bars, focused listening to the F♮ is needed to keep the melody to the fore while the harmonies change subtly underneath, resolving to the final, contented C major chord.

B:4 J. F. F. Burgmüller *Refrain du gondolier (Gondolier's Song)*

The image of a gondolier serenading a loving couple is familiar to us, yet probably less so for many pupils. A pupil may need help picturing Venice, therefore, if this lilting barcarolle is to be performed with conviction. It might be worth looking at one of the Venetian Gondola Songs from Mendelssohn's *Songs without Words* for comparison, and possibly watching something of Venice on film.

The song itself is of greatest importance and should seduce the listener with its beauty, sound and subtlety. Putting words to the melody will really help give it musical shape, and show where it needs to 'breathe'. In this sense bar 6 would benefit from a little time across the first four quavers and a slight breath before beginning the next phrase. It is important not to get too fussy about the marks of articulation: the staccato dots imply only a gently detached line with the held pedal – a different colour from a legato line with pedal. Tenuto marks are pointers towards the rubato you might use, while the *sforzando* should be expressive, not violent.

A flexible and sensitive accompaniment – allowing the rubato the tune needs and following rather than leading – should support the natural eloquence and pliancy of the melody. Much will depend upon the control of the rising arpeggio figures. The accompaniment may interfere as it gets closer in register to the melodic line, so the left hand's upper notes should be particularly quiet, the bass note a little fuller to support the harmony.

The wonderful, caressing semiquavers (bar 27 and similar) need time for control and to avoid sounding too frantic. The grace notes should be gentle and unhurried and, despite fingering suggesting the opposite, the trill in bar 30 could sound better if begun on the note.

Pedal must be used throughout, not just where marked. Again, staccato dots on the bass notes are not 'staccato' but markings to indicate that the hand jumps. *Una corda* in bar 31 will enhance the repeat, and careful changes of the damper pedal will colour the last line as will a sensitively judged ritardando and placing of the final chord.

B:5 Esplá *Canción de cuna (Cradle Song)*

A light touch is required in this dreamy yet unusual lullaby, for which the player must calm and lull the listener without fuss, with a beauty of line and consummate technical ease. The ABA structure is self-evident, but the wonderful change to B major in the middle section is unexpected – the child transported briefly to another world, before waking from the dream in a lovely codetta and returning to the cradle song.

Textural balance, a fleetness of fingers and the fluency to enable the subtlest of rubato are all needed to enhance the lullaby. The balance problems exist not just between the hands but also within the right hand. The opening must have a soft underlying harmony, the tune to the fore. This can be achieved with the hand weighted to the outside and a light, controlled thumb. All the harmony notes should be held meticulously so that, for instance, the E in bar 1 sounds across the bar-line and can be caught with the pedal change.

The pedalling needs careful consideration: too much will lead to a mush of sound, too little and the piece will sound decidedly dry. Much depends upon the instrument and room, but pedalling each bar with a quick (and quiet!) pedal change on the fourth quaver beat (or change of harmony) will work for most of the opening section. In the middle section it's more appropriate to pedal each crotchet beat.

Fingers need to be light and agile, particularly through the grace notes, which should be controlled, delightfully articulated and on the beat. On the few left-hand stretches (bars 18 and 52), the lowest note should be played on the beat together with the right hand, the second note following on.

The performance cries out for instinctive ebb and flow and delicate musical features. To convey the character, consider a subtle contrast from *pianissimo* to *pianississimo*, an expressive *subito pianissimo* at the key change, and giving time at the poignant G♯ in bar 23, on the pauses and through the ritardandos.

Finally, there is a probable misprint in bar 45, which almost certainly should be the same as bar 3.

B:6 Mendelssohn *Song without Words*

This is a typically beautiful Mendelssohn song, tinged with sadness and tenderness. Its poetry will only surface, though, with sensitive playing; it needs a singer's instinctive ear for shaping a melody and an accompanist's ear for balance.

In the opening, the lower notes of the left hand's accompaniment provide a counter-melody, almost a duet part. Playing this together with the principal melody until the hands are working in sympathy would be a good place to start; only after this should the repeated Es and Ds of the left hand be added – over-holding the lower bass notes as well to enable a more flexible use of pedal. The repeated notes must be subtly controlled to avoid becoming intrusive.

There are added difficulties where the right hand has to take the accompaniment as well as the melody (e.g. bars 17 and 18), and detailed technical work will be needed here to avoid too thick a texture. The focus of this work should be on voicing the top note while keeping the semiquavers light, unaccented and seamless, with a relaxed arm.

The melody itself needs long phrases and an understanding of their direction – their rise, fall and context. The first phrase, for instance, is eight bars long, but conveying this while retaining the shape of the smaller phrases and 'sighs' within requires a subtlety of tone control. There is a small crescendo to a gentle *sforzando* in bar 3 or 4 (depending on the edition you use), though the phrase feels as if it should go to bar 4. Whatever your musical judgement here, the repeated Fs require conscientious shaping away from or towards the *sforzando.* It is worth writing in extra dynamics throughout the piece to define the pupil's intentions.

Pedalling should be carefully chosen. Depending on the instrument, try frequent small changes, using just the top of the pedal, to give warmth yet avoid muddy texture or dissonant clashes of harmony. The more the hands can do to hold the counter-melodies, the more the pedal can be changed without losing texture.

Certain articulation and dynamics deserve special mention. *Sforzandos* should always be warmly interpreted, never harshly, and the staccato dots simply signify repeated notes, and are certainly not dry of pedal. The *forte* at the end should not be too rigorous; in context it is simply a moment of drama, and the final pause an indication that the hands are not to move from above the key until all the resonance is gone from the room.

C:1 Richard Rodney Bennett *Four Calling Birds*

This charming movement from Bennett's *Partridge Pie* collection has something of the motion and feeling of a gentle waltz, rather along the lines of a Satie *Gymnopédie*. The metronome mark yields a suitably leisurely tempo, but it is possible to go fractionally faster, up to crotchet = *c*.88, without losing the 'peaceful, distant' effect. The tempo is modified in several places by either *poco rit.* or *sost.*, and any undue exaggeration of tempo change can be avoided by leaving most of the slowing down or sustaining of the sound to the ends of the bars in question. This will also allow for a slightly more substantial slowing down at the very end.

The notes lie very comfortably under the hands and present no serious technical challenge, but the 'birdsong' grace notes need real clarity, and staccato practice may help to achieve this, even though the final effect will be smoother and gentler. Indeed, awkwardness or angularity should be avoided, and the most graceful performances will not rush through the grace notes but will allow them their melodically decorative function, placing them before the beat.

The single specific pedal marking, at bar 34, requires the resonance to last for two bars. However, there is a *con ped.* indication at the start of the piece, and performances will benefit from appropriate use of pedal throughout, mainly on a bar-by-bar basis.

The dynamic markings are most frequently *piano* or *mezzo-piano*, and even the solitary *forte* is qualified by *ma dolce*, suggesting that the sound should be achieved by arm weight rather than brute force! In any case, the passage running from bar 32 to bar 44 will need a sense of melodic projection, with the arm weight seemingly channelled down the outer fingers of the right hand. A slight rightward tilting of the forearm may help to achieve the desired voicing, which will also aid the moulding of the long phrases.

A successful performance of this piece needs a siren-like seductiveness, perhaps resembling the alluring song of a call-bird rather than the Four *Calling* Birds!

C:2 Paul Harvey *Rumba Toccata*

Combining the exciting technical features of a toccata with the rumba's infectious rhythms, this is a real 'fun' piece – fun to play and fun to listen to.

The piece is beautifully conceived for the keyboard, although initially it will be necessary to work out precisely which hand does what and when. The left hand has most of the moving around and leaping, while the right hand copes with the repeated notes. The printed fingering works well, but in bar 28 you may like to try using 3-1-2-1 in the right hand above 1-2-3-5 in the left, and in bars 46–8, try using 1-2-4 in the left with, in the right, 2/1 on the final semiquaver chord of each bar. Whatever is decided, the touch needs to be precise throughout, played from the fingertip and with a real edge to the sound.

Although the tempo marking is *Presto agitato*, the metronome mark is, in fact, not especially fast. The piece calls for a regular but cumulative momentum rather than for scrambling; in such music as this, the former is always more thrilling than the latter. No rubato or ritenuto is required, but the left hand should have a sense of rhythmic 'play' to capture the dance flavour. Notice also that some of the left-hand part is notated in semiquavers but that quavers are in the majority, suggesting that they serve a melodic function. The semiquavers are also the notes requiring the most attack (marked *forte*), so the touch can be shorter and sharper on these, but very slightly deeper and more sustained on the quavers.

Although the music is lively, it is not especially loud, with *forte* being the most forceful dynamic marking. This also accords with the sense of playfulness in the music, and examiners will enjoy performances that can project this aspect, more than those that are relentlessly mechanical. In fact, in a really successful performance of this piece, the listener should find it hard to sit still.

C:3 Lhotka-Kalinski *Microforms*

This colourful set of miniatures, evoking birdsong, will appeal to pupils with more sophisticated tastes and who enjoy responding to musical challenges.

The musical challenges are certainly uppermost in these pieces, because the player's technique is not greatly stretched. Perhaps the requirement simultaneously to sustain and release notes in the same hand, as found especially in piece III, bars 7–8, will be a new feature to some pupils, but the use of a good fingering, such as that marked in the score, will solve any potential problems. Also in piece III, a change of fingers on the demisemiquaver repeated notes may give greater clarity.

Careful counting in the earliest learning stages of all four pieces will be needed. It would be a good idea to feel the music in quaver units with the metronome set respectively to quaver = 120, 96, 132 and 120, clapping out the rhythms to this regular pulse. This groundwork needs to be assimilated before a more 'artistic' interpretation can convincingly emerge. In due course, a slow, flexible pulse, according to the metre marked in the score, will allow the music its expressive potential.

Where interpretative aspects are concerned, the composer has supplied detailed dynamics and articulative instructions, and these should be observed closely. The absence of pedal markings suggests a predominantly dry texture (as does the imitation of birdsong), but a judicious application of pedal may help passages that invite a more sustained quality, as in piece I, bar 2 and piece III, bars 1–6 (changing each beat), or where connection between chords in the left hand seems desirable, as in piece IV.

The loudest dynamic of *mezzo-forte* is infrequent and never sustained for long, so these pieces are ideal territory for exploring levels of *mezzo-piano, piano* and *pianissimo.* Where this last is indicated, the addition of the *una corda* pedal will yield an appropriate tonal colour. The *sforzando* in piece IV should be restrained and in proportion with the surrounding *mezzo-piano* and *piano* markings.

These pieces are well worth the effort and their appeal grows with acquaintance. If pupils enjoy the experience, they could try listening to some of Messiaen's birdsong-inspired music.

C:4 Avril Anderson *A Story Untold*

This piece will suit pupils whose fingers are not especially dextrous but who can play with emphatic clarity and secure rhythm. Many will be familiar with this idiom having played Bartók's music; others may need to accustom themselves to its sound-world.

The great Sviatoslav Richter once stated that he was against performers 'interpreting' a work. Here, the composer has written most of the 'interpretation' into the score, thereby making the performance of the piece relatively straightforward.

A steady rhythmic drive is of the essence in this music. With much of the writing in one or two parts, tapping out the right- and left-hand rhythms may be a useful preliminary exercise in coming to grips with both the interlocking hand positions and the shifting metres. When introducing the notes, be aware that much of the writing involves mirror patterns, but occasionally this changes to similar-motion, as at bar 21 and bars 30–32.

The composer instructs that evenness of touch between the hands is required, and a firm forearm-to-finger action should enable this. Ideally, the examiner should not be able to hear that the material is passing from one hand to the other. A 'beautiful tone' is certainly not called for; instead, a dry, percussive sound is suitable, with pedal applied only where marked.

There is no need to be timid where dynamics are concerned since the piece is marked mainly *forte.* Changes to and from the lower dynamic levels may be done abruptly to create a 'terraced' effect, with only one brief crescendo being required at bar 24. Articulation should be detached, apart from where slur or phrase marks have been added, and a sense of where the stronger parts of the metre fall is needed if the piece is not to end up sounding like a string of equalized, undifferentiated events.

Overall, a slightly stubborn, reluctant quality mixed with a dash of wry humour will help to project the mood. Indeed, the narrator's stubbornness may be what is preventing this story from being told!

C:5 Octavio Pinto *Run, Run!*

This brilliant, toccata-like piece will appeal to the extroverts among your pupils and is an exciting addition to that repertoire of works that sound harder than they actually are!

In the outer sections of this piece, the obvious technical challenge is to achieve a slick and even alternation between the hands. Forearms and wrists need to be relaxed and supple; focusing on a down-up sensation rather than lateral movement should guard against tension. Fingering all triads 5-3-1 in each hand will work throughout, but larger hands may appreciate relief from this by fingering the lower of any adjacent triads with 2-4-5 in the left hand and 4-2-1 in the right.

In music that has a motoric quality, as is found in these outer sections, the temptation to hammer and to hurry needs to be resisted. A metronome setting of crotchet = *c.*112 will launch a suitable tempo, although pliant wrists may comfortably go faster. But whatever speed is chosen, it needs to be stable. Notice also that the dynamic level never rises above *mezzo-forte,* indicating that excitement is generated by understatement rather than by overstatement.

The inexplicable appearance of the organ-grinder gives the middle section an almost surreal quality, which needs to be reflected by a reversal of mood. Here the music should be carefully voiced to bring out the melody and to keep the right hand's accompanying 3rds subdued. To preserve a legato line in bars 38–9 and 42–3, the right-hand fifth finger can be tucked under the fourth where marked. (If your pupil has not encountered this technique before, try getting him or her to play a descending scale with alternating fifth and fourth fingers!)

The organ-grinder episode will also benefit from the use of pedal; where unmarked, applying pedal throughout the bar, changing on the first beat, will work (perhaps surprisingly), although the deft-footed may wish to slip in some extra changes in the more chromatic parts.

By means of a well-judged diminuendo and a finely measured glissando, the listener can imagine our runner disappearing into the distance – but with no loss of speed.

C:6 Prokofiev *Valse*

Although this piece seems to evoke the Viennese waltz idiom, it is also full of the composer's typical playful irony. Coming from a set of pieces entitled *Musique d'enfants*, it offers the image perhaps of two children practising the dance, losing the lilt once or twice, occasionally getting a little behind (in the *poco rit.* bars), parodying their own efforts in the middle section and then running off to do something else at the end.

Technically, one of the principal challenges is the safe negotiation of the left-hand leaps. In each case the first, lower note will need to be the springboard from which the upper two-note chord is gauged. This can be practised on its own, slowly, firstly looking at the hand and then looking away from it so that the motion becomes habitual. In the right hand, it may be helpful to finger the three-quaver, dotted-crotchet pattern in bars 16–17 and 54–5 with a 2-3-1-5 arrangement, which can helpfully be mirrored simultaneously in the left.

Prokofiev's patterning of the left-hand part, with its downbeat bass note, is useful in creating a one-in-a-bar feeling and, in this respect, a tempo of dotted minim = *c.*50 supplies an appropriately supportive tempo. In line with this, pedal may be applied to the first beats only of bars 1–8 but thereafter will need to be adapted. For example, in bars 13–16 and 51–4 longer pedals, changing only between each bar, will work, and one pedal can be applied to the first and second beats during bars 25–36.

The middle section (bars 25–40) loses the waltz lilt a little, suggesting greater equalization of the metre's three beats, but accompanying quavers should not intrude and the fingers need to be kept close to the keys. The third beats need to be short and light with no suggestion of an offbeat accent. Dynamics never rise above *mezzo-forte*, and a light, if deliberate, touch is required throughout.

Examiners will naturally appreciate accuracy and precision in a performance of this piece, but will be even more impressed if they feel that an 'invitation to the dance' has occurred.

GRADE 7

The final grades should be equally rewarding to teachers, pupils and parents, whose involvement in the exams should be bearing fruit. The playing usually sounds quite accomplished even at a pass level, while merit and distinction categories will acknowledge musical and polished performances of real artistic quality. The highest marks most frequently go to candidates choosing pieces within their own technical comfort zone, so that expressive details and communication can lift the music off the page.

A:1 John Loeillet *Giga*

This lively music should appeal to all tastes, but will especially suit the more extrovert student. It also requires fingers that are strong and disciplined, if not especially dextrous.

A tempo of dotted crotchet = 116 works well, yielding a pace fast enough to capture the dance character, but also one that allows the ornaments to be comfortably assimilated. Despite the need for firm, agile fingers when executing the ornaments, it can be helpful to imagine that there is plenty of time for them (which there is!), thereby according these stylistic features an expressive rather than irruptive role.

Generally there is a four-in-a-bar feeling, with primary emphasis on beat one and secondary emphasis on beat three. If this pattern is achieved, it will highlight those places where it changes, as in, for example, bars 3–4 and 49–50, where emphasizing beats two and four provides rhythmic interest and variety. Naturally, these emphases need to be subtly conveyed in order to avoid musical overstatement and distortion.

The score typically shows no dynamics, but the music does offer some possibilities. For example, the climbing passages at bars 3–4 and 21–2 seem to invite a crescendo, while melodic repetition, such as in bars 19–21 and 54–5, may benefit from an 'echo' effect. Where the energetic chordal textures at bars 9 and 12 suggest a robust (but not ugly) *forte*, the running quavers lead each half to a quiet conclusion.

The articulation needs to be clean and precise. An all-staccato account is probably best avoided, although the dotted-crotchet chords in the left hand may be slightly separated. Mixed articulation in the right hand is likely to produce the most interesting musical results. For example, consider phrasing in groups of three between the second half of bar 14 through bar 15; phrasing could be slurred couplets plus a staccato third quaver during bars 16–18; and there might be a continuous legato in bars 19–21. At no point need there be any sense of the finger lingering on the key, except on the final right-hand chord of each half.

Whatever your final dynamic and choice of articulation, it is worth remembering Türk's advice that a giga 'is executed in a somewhat short and light fashion. Its character is for the most part one of cheerfulness.'

A:2 Beethoven *Allegretto in C minor*

Those pupils with a sense of drama will really take to this piece. It contains a huge dynamic and emotional range, yet all within a relatively short time-span.

An appropriate speed is vital for a stylish reading, and dotted minim = *c.*72 gives a sensible mean, creating a one-in-a-bar feeling and guarding against too 'syllabic' an approach. It will also help to underline the rhythmic 'dislocation' of the hemiolas in the passage beginning bar 40 and again from 136. The 'correction' of this feature, at bar 144 in particular, can be most assertive. No significant modification of the tempo is needed, except at bar 151 where the music is marked *mancando,* which indicates a gradual reduction of tempo and dynamic.

The tempo does not generate any very fast fingerwork, but to avoid any sense of rushing, control of the quaver motion is important. Good fingering will help, and in bars 30 and 126 you may like to try a descending right-hand pattern: 2-4-1-5-3-5, placing 5 on the final D of the next bar, thus enabling 2 to land on the subsequent A♭. Familiarization with the 'geography' of the left hand in bars 81–5 demands careful, possibly single-handed, practice, but the last leap to the octave Bs may become easier if the right-hand thumb takes the left hand's final quaver of bar 84; the same D is then taken by the third finger of the right hand at the beginning of the next bar.

Beethoven added very few dynamic markings to this score, so you may find the editorial suggestions helpful. However, the *fortissimo* markings in bars 33, 129 and 144 are the composer's own, and in the first two of these, the left arm will need to execute a weighty, but relaxed, downwards motion. Consider the right hand's dynamic level here as a single *forte* – achieved via a contained forearm rotary movement in which, for a tidy result, the fingers are not lifted too high above the keys.

Phrasing in the major section (from bar 48) needs to be smooth, especially in the left hand. Using the fourth finger on the third beats of bars

49–51, left hand, may help, and in bars 65–70 fingering the descending five-note patterns 1-2-3-4-5 could aid the creation of a smooth, even line.

Examiners will particularly enjoy performances that convey the music's tension and release, and the inherent character of its contrasting elements.

A:3 W. F. Bach *Polonaise No. 5 in E flat*

Bold and assertive, this Polonaise will suit players with strong fingers and a secure grasp of rhythm. Performances of this dance should have a measured tread and a clear sense of moving towards the first beat of the bar.

Crotchet = *c*.54 suggests a deliberate pace, and one which renders the passagework manageable by most Grade 7 players. More nimble fingers could probably cope with a slightly faster tempo. The intricacies of the timing will require some careful preliminary unravelling, since the music provides many opportunities for confusing quaver with semiquaver speeds, or semiquaver with demisemiquaver speeds!

The tricky technical features are made easier by using good hand and finger arrangements. In bars 13–16, for example, the last three semiquaver chords can be distributed so that 2/1 in the right hand takes the upper two notes of the first of the chords, and the thumb the top note of the next one. The left hand thus takes, progressively, one, two, then three notes. In other words, hands may follow the written note distribution across staves rather than the beaming and connecting stems. Also, the left hand may take all notes at the beginning of bars 6 and 30, remembering to release the quaver in time. To ease the strain of the *pralltriller* in bars 19 and 20, the right hand's lowest note under the trill may be omitted without upsetting the harmony.

The composer provided a number of articulation and dynamic indications, with the latter generally polarized. Making a sharp distinction between *forte* and *piano* levels will effectively highlight those places where hairpins call for graded dynamics. However, even the quiet end of the range needs a degree of firmness, and both soft and loud will benefit from clear articulation, perhaps with a suggestion of nervous tension in the sound (though not in the arms!). This tone quality might be mellowed by the application of pedal on one or two occasions, such as in bars 11 and 35 (changing with the quavers) or on the third beats of bars 13–16. In contrast, the often-repeated dactylic figures in the left hand, such as those in bars 19–20, need an alert, springy quality to help convey the character.

The most successful candidates will not only negotiate the notes comfortably – and in time – but will project the work's buoyancy and slightly blustering good humour.

A:4 Clementi *Allegro assai*

This engaging sonata movement will appeal to pupils blessed with a good ear for articulation, texture and, perhaps most importantly, musical dialogue.

The music can usefully be thought of as a rondo (especially when played without the repeat), fulfilling an ABACA format. An idea of the movement's design may be communicated in performance by extending the quaver rests in bars 20 and 82 by the merest whisker, to mark the conclusion of the A sections and the introduction of the episodes.

Although *allegro assai* is often translated as 'very fast', it might be safer to think of *assai* as indicating 'enough', bearing in mind that demisemiquavers have to be cleanly enunciated at several places in the right hand and that the regular left-hand Alberti figurations need to be properly controlled. A metronome mark of dotted crotchet = 80 yields an appropriate tempo, preserving a sense of one-in-a-bar but without generating undue urgency.

Firm fingertips, close to the keys, governed by no more than a hint of wrist rotation, should keep the Alberti patterns under control, supporting rather than engulfing the right-hand parts. It is probably advisable to arrange your pupil's fingering so that the demisemiquavers in bars 17–18 and later are played with a 2-3-4-3 arrangement, thereby reducing reliance on weaker fingers.

Contrast is an essential feature of the music, and examiners will appreciate performances that project this. The staccatos should be crisp and rhythmically placed, while the slurred right-hand quavers of bars 10–12 and similar need to extend beyond the division of the bar to be part of a far longer phrase. The left hand's leaping quavers will benefit from staccato execution.

Musical dialogue is clearly reflected in the marked dynamics. Throughout bars 1–82 (ABA) one can imagine 'the voice of reason' in patient conversation with 'the voice of rebellion'. Perhaps a third, more compromising, voice enters the scene in bars 83–132; here the *forte* markings in bars 99, 101, 103 and 105 seem to represent emphasis rather than noise, and those from 111 to the end of the section may be bold rather than clamorous. The dynamics from bar 133 to the end can be deduced from similar passages earlier in the movement.

The technical demands of this piece are well within the boundaries of the grade, and only with the play of imaginative musical ideas will the music really be brought to life.

A:5 Haydn *Finale (Presto)*

This lively finale from Haydn's Sonata in A flat, Hob. XVI/46 has, despite hints of sterner undercurrents, an overall good humour, which requires a sparkling freshness of sound.

The tempo should be fast, but an over-ambitious pace may turn the music into an uncomfortable scramble. Remember that a Presto in the Classical period implied less velocity than more recent usage would indicate; a metronome mark of crotchet = *c.*130 will probably generate the appropriate momentum.

The runs need a firm (but not hard) touch; playing from the tip of the finger, rather than the pad, may help to generate the necessary clarity and brilliance. For controlled execution and avoiding splashiness, the see-sawing semiquavers in bars 29–36 and similar demand a flexible wrist within a compact rotational movement. This technique will require practice at slow speed, and with differing degrees of arm weight so that varied dynamic levels can be cultivated.

Any editorial suggestions for dynamics on your score may be helpful, but given that Haydn's score seems to have been 'clean' in this respect, there is no need to feel restricted. Nevertheless, dynamics reflecting melodic contours or the tension and release of the music are necessary if a candidate is to show awareness of style. For example, the rapid modulations in bars 46–53 and bars 73–82 create a harmonic intensification which can be expressed through a crescendo, and echo effects can be applied between bars 21 and 25 (also bars 111 and 115) wherein the second phrase is a repetition of the first. Such features may also give clues to the surrounding dynamics. A strong sound is called for in places, perhaps even at the start, but this should always be a refined *forte*, never a percussive one.

Articulation can help bring the music to life and, generally, a light staccato will aid the many anacrusis quavers as well as the leaping left-hand figures in places such as bars 30–37 and 69–81. The music does not demand pedal use anywhere; touches may, however, be applied to even out repeated semiquaver pitches (in the right hand of bars 3–4, e.g), as well as to give warmth to the semiquaver runs in stretches such as bars 46–52 and 100–105 – where its light application to the second beat of each bar may guard against excessive dryness.

This piece is ideal for a pupil who has obedient, nimble fingers, and who can hold a steady pulse but also convey humour and drama.

A:6 D. Scarlatti *Sonata in C*

Performances of this sparkling sonata, with its gigue-like character, need dancing fingers anchored by a rock-steady pulse. A tempo in the region of dotted crotchet = 102 should generate an appropriate combination of dash and poise.

One of the piece's technical challenges lies in the ornaments, which need deftness of execution if they are, in the words of C. P. E. Bach, 'to enliven the tones'. The mordents should probably begin on the upper note, but if your pupil has difficulty fitting four notes into the available time, a three-note mordent, starting on the principal note, will achieve a similar effect. Most importantly, the tempo must not be delayed nor the melodic line disrupted. The appoggiaturas should almost certainly be executed as acciaccaturas, and a free, downward movement of the forearm will achieve a gentle emphasis of the stronger beats, accommodating both grace note and main note within a single physical gesture. The right-hand leaps in bars 19 and 20 (which may be mimicked, if desired, in bars 58 and 59) need to be judged carefully if the upper note is to be kept light. Memory work may help here.

On matters of articulation, it must be remembered that while an edition may contain some helpful suggestions, Scarlatti's text contains no performance directions; players are free to make their own choices. Mixed articulations are likely to produce the most interesting musical results. For example, a legato–staccato articulation of the crotchet–quaver (trochaic) figures which occur throughout, especially in the left hand, will work well, while downward-leaping arpeggiations will benefit from a fully staccato touch, executed from a well-sprung wrist via the fingertips. The phrasing works across the bar-lines, so pupils should treat phrase openings (often the fifth quaver of the bar) lightly, so that the phrase can be directed towards its peak, which is sometimes signalled by an ornament.

It is a good idea to keep the general dynamic level fairly light so as to preserve musical buoyancy. However, crescendos suggest themselves at places where repetition occurs, as in bars 14–16 and 18–20, or where there is harmonic and textural intensification, as in bars 34–41. The flourish at bar 42, in which this passage culminates, can be played in time; but it might be more effective if performed freely, perhaps applying a pause to the low Gs.

Successful performances of this sonata can provide an exhilarating opening to a Grade 7 programme, clearing away any cobwebs that may have accumulated in the examination room!

B:1 Sibelius *Landscape*

The *Five Sketches,* Op. 114 evoke images of the beautiful countryside of Sibelius's native Finland. Forests and lakes are referred to in some of the titles, but with just 'Landscape' to prompt the imagination, we must allow the music itself to suggest the scene.

With its changing note-values, keys and time signatures, the music looks complicated, even daunting, on the page. To avoid the possibility of learning incorrect rhythms or notes, then, it would be wise to have a good practice plan. Firstly, practise the 'bare bones' of the rhythm. Counting crotchet beats, work steadily through the piece, playing the groups of semiquavers and demisemiquavers that are accompanying figures (bars 4, 8 and similar) in block chords. This not only avoids the danger of slowing the tempo as faster notes appear, it helps prepare the hand for the shape of each group and makes rippling through fearful-looking demisemiquavers positively enjoyable!

The first theme moves steadily into the fourth bar and to the long tied chord. As with all the other points of repose, it should not be hurried nor its length cut short. It is as though the eye dwells upon some point of interest in the landscape.

The next theme – from bar 5 – is fragmented at first, before being carried along by the flowing semiquaver accompaniment (starting on the last beat of bar 7). This left-hand pattern will be more secure if played throughout using 5-3-2-1 and, as already suggested, practised first in block chords. By the time the restatement of the first theme is reached at bar 13, almost all the different rhythms have been encountered, and already the music has passed from E flat major, through G flat major and B major, to arrive in E major! The enharmonic and side-stepping key changes continue, reflecting different aspects of mood and scenery, so it would be wise to keep checking and rechecking the notes as the piece is learnt.

Pedal is only marked in a few places, where special effects are required, but legato pedalling will be needed throughout the piece. The very long pedal in bars 33–8 will require careful balancing: the rippling right-hand figures should be quite subdued, with only a modest crescendo and diminuendo as they rise and fall towards the final cadence.

Throughout, there are just a few moments of silence. The rests in bars 5, 6 and 7 (and corresponding places in the second half) should make a telling contribution to the atmosphere of this demanding but hauntingly beautiful piece.

B:2 Smetana *Album Leaf*

The challenge in this sparkling *moto perpetuo* is to reveal the musical detail within the constant flow of semiquavers. There is a danger that it could sound like a finger exercise. Agile fingers are essential but so, too, will be tone control and rhythmic interest.

First look at the dynamic marks. Beginning *piano*, a gradual crescendo from bar 8 arrives at *forte* in bar 13. From bar 17 a sweeter, quieter tone is explored, so do not be afraid to employ the *una corda* pedal occasionally. These changes in colour continue throughout the piece.

The left hand plays a supporting role but is almost more important than the right. The staccato should be light and buoyant, but the accents clearly marked and notes given full value. This rhythmic punctuation will bring vitality and impetus to the semiquavers. The left hand has to negotiate some wide jumps, and it might be safer on occasion to take notes with the right hand. For instance, in the first bar the right hand could play the first chord's B and D with first and second fingers, leaving the left hand with a single note and only an octave jump; the same applies to first beats of bars 5 and 9. If you adopt this idea, the notated fingering must be adapted before any serious practice begins.

From bar 49 further interest is created in the right hand by a shift of emphasis to the fourth semiquaver of each beat. Here the staccato marks should be regarded as a type of accent and, as these notes are picked out, a curving, offbeat melody appears over the top. Begin this passage by practising the first two notes (D and E) as a slow trill, using thumb and second finger. Once this feels easy and the arm is balanced comfortably behind these fingers, begin to include the other notes, extending the hand and allowing the forearm to rotate outwards slightly. After firmly tapping the melody note, let the hand relax again and the arm resume its balanced position. Where the interval opens up beyond an octave, a larger lateral arm movement is required. Later, at bar 69, the same figure is further complicated by having to hold down the upper melody notes while the lower notes begin to move about. Slow practice will help to secure this passage.

Although not indicated in the score, a *poco ritenuto* through bars 77 and 78 makes musical sense. Having arrived on the final chord, there should be a moment's pause before beginning the gradual *accel.* and *dim.* to the end.

B:3 Tchaikovsky *Octobre: Chant d'automne*

In countries where the climate is as varied as it is in Russia, the seasons have a profound influence upon people's lives and moods. In *October: Song of Autumn* Tchaikovsky expresses feelings of regret as memories of summer fade and winter approaches.

A successful performance will depend not only on skilful pedalling and a convincing rubato, but also on beautiful tone. Use a relaxed but well-supported arm to mould the melodic lines, feeling the weight passing from finger to finger. Remember that it is the dynamic level of the accompaniment that determines how loud or quiet a passage sounds. Even in the quietest phrase, the melody must have sufficient tone to 'sing'. At bar 9 (marcato) the principal melody passes to the left hand. This is a typical inner melody where the thumb plays many of the notes, and it may help if the right hand takes some of them, perhaps the first B♭ in bar 11; the E, D and C♯ in bar 12; the C at bar 15. This is as much to do with the management of the pedal as with the spacing of the notes.

Pedal is marked in many places, but should be used almost throughout. As long as it is changed on crotchet beats where the harmony moves quickly, or where the melody has quaver movement, there will be no build-up of dissonance. It is most important that the bass line is sustained to give support to the texture.

Counter-melodies play a significant part in Tchaikovsky's music, and at bar 9 the right hand begins to weave beautiful shapes above the main theme. When trying to balance all the textural strands, your pupil might think of different instruments; for instance, the cellos might have the main tune and an oboe the counter-melody, while muted strings provide the background. Accents such as those in bars 8 and 24 should be 'leaned on' as though they are sighs, and the notes marked with lines (bar 5 etc.) are best played by dropping from slightly above the key.

At bar 17 the melancholy of D minor briefly gives way to a more optimistic F major, and the phrases grow steadily towards a spread chord and pause in bar 21. The notes of this chord might be redistributed between the hands, leaving the top note to be taken by the left hand. Back in the minor again, the falling, fragmented melody lines are rich in chromaticism and full of anguish.

After the da capo repeat has been played, bar 16 links to the coda, and this may need practice. There is an air of resignation in the final bars, and the *una corda* pedal will help to fade the music into silence.

B:4 Bruch *Swedish Dance in F minor*

This stately Swedish Dance stays almost entirely in the melancholy key of F minor, with only a brief glimpse of A flat major in the middle section.

As with all dances, it is important to discover where the strong beats lie and to feel the rhythmic ebb and flow. In ABA form, this dance appears to be composed in simple four-bar phrases, but in the outer sections the strong beat is rarely on the first beat of the bar. In fact, each phrase may be heard as three bars of quadruple time instead of the notated four bars of triple. To establish this flow through the bar-lines to each point of repose, play just the right hand, counting four instead of three as you do so. However, do then revert to counting in three, otherwise the desired syncopated effect may be weakened.

The middle section is in strict triple time, with definite first-beat accents, thus making an effective contrast. For the sake of the overall shape of the dance, candidates will be forgiven for playing this section with the repeat, as marked. A slight break at the end of both the first and second bars of this new figure will help to emphasize its lilting rhythm. It will also allow time to spread the left-hand chords and catch the bass note (F) with the pedal.

In the first section several spread chords have to be negotiated. In bar 5, a similar tiny break before the first chord works well, but a break is not desirable for the next chord in that bar. Here, it would be better to play the bass note (B♭) with the right-hand chord (changing the pedal at the same time), and then gently fill in the other notes (F and D♭) before playing the right-hand octave D♭. Yet another solution is required for the next two spread chords, in bars 6–7. The pedal will have to be changed slightly early if the bass notes are to be caught, and a small break will occur between the melody D♭ and C (bar 6). However, at the next pedal change the slurred melody across the bar-line can remain legato if the fourth finger is used on the A♭ quaver and the third finger on the F.

In the final section the right hand is almost the same as that of the opening section, but the left hand and pedal will require practice before there is an easy flow. Here the bass notes (some of which have crotchet stems) need a rich sonority while the semiquavers ripple more lightly in order to support the beautiful cantabile melody.

B:5 Chopin *Mazurka in B flat*

It is always a joy to begin to play some of the pieces from the concert repertoire, and the music of Chopin holds a very special place in the hearts of pianists and audiences alike. Of the three main dances that Chopin composed – the polonaise, mazurka and waltz – the mazurka is the most elusive. As with almost every form Chopin adopted, this rustic Polish dance was moulded into his own, very personal style.

Chopin wrote mazurkas throughout his life; they were among the first pieces he composed, and the last. When he played them himself, it was said that they sounded as though they were written in duple or quadruple time because of his very unusual rubato. The best way of discovering this characteristic rhythm is to listen to great pianists, preferably Polish, such as Artur Rubinstein.

A quick look at the structure of the piece will help to show how the music ebbs and flows. The first phrase presses forward a little towards the third bar where the trill could be slightly lengthened before tipping into the playful answering phrase. Four more bars complete the principal theme, which is then repeated. Almost every bar begins with a dotted rhythm (with or without a semiquaver rest), and it should always be very crisp. A slight stretching of the first note in bars 7, 8 and 11 will suggest the feeling of duple time that Chopin conveyed – without significantly adding to the bar.

Beginning at bars 25 and 45 respectively, the two contrasting themes of this rondo-like form have the tempo fluctuations written into the score (*stretto, poco rall.* and *rubato*). The first theme is marked *legato* and has more pairs of equal quavers than elsewhere, so it should be made altogether smoother than the principal theme. The second theme is a remarkable contrast. The wailing augmented 2nds, diminished 5ths and 9ths of this 'gypsy' melody are set against a dissonant drone bass that pre-empts Bartók's own treatment of folk music by some eighty years. Marked *sotto voce,* the section would benefit from using the *una corda* pedal. It is this tune, above all, that can be lingered over and expressively shaped until it is swept away by the return of the irrepressible principal theme.

B:6 Schumann *Träumerei (Dreaming)*

With a piece as familiar as Schumann's 'Dreaming' we tend to forget just what makes it so special. By rediscovering it for ourselves we can take pleasure in sharing its beauties with our pupils.

The miracle of this seemingly simple piece is that it is built from a rising six-note figure that, with almost every repetition, leads to a different harmony, often by means of a different interval. Each change expresses a new mood. The opening phrase, with its shift from chord I to chord IV, is warm and reassuring, but the second leads to a surprising dominant 7th, foreign to the home key. This casts radiance on the phrase, before sinking through D minor and some chromatic harmony to the key of C major.

The approach intervals add to the colour of each phrase – the first a perfect 4th, the second a major 6th and then a crushing minor 3rd (bar 10) that prepares the way for a dominant minor 9th chord, and chromatic drift down into the sad key of G minor. After a brief excursion to B flat major, the theme returns in its original guise in the home key. However, Schumann has yet another trick up his sleeve. The final statement – and the piece's climax – rises to a glowing dominant *major* 9th, as though moving into C major again, only to fall back into the final cadence and a deep, dreamless sleep. Many pianists find it easier and musically more effective to arpeggiate this wide-spanning climax chord, thus delaying, and giving emphasis to, the melody note.

When preparing this piece, there are two main technical considerations. First there must be a lovely singing tone, and the melody moulded so that its special shape is heard. A gentle crescendo carries the first half of the phrase to its highest point, but then it falls back by means of three four-note curves to its final note. These undulating fragments are an important feature and must be carefully shaped, especially when they pass through the texture towards the bass. The second technical consideration is the pedalling. Sooner or later a pianist must learn how to catch the bass note of a spread chord. The pedal should be changed as the bass note is played, but it is often left until the chord is completed, thus losing the most important note of the harmony. When managed correctly, a slight gap usually occurs in the melody line, but in this piece the melody note can be held through the pedal-change because it is common to both chords (bar 2, for instance).

C:1 Naji Hakim *Dumia*

Pupils are often surprisingly receptive to modern classical styles, especially when they are introduced in an imaginative way. Middle Eastern folk-style pervades this unusual piece, and although it might look daunting, its musical attractiveness and sheer athleticism make it well worth the effort.

An initial glance will reveal some repetition of ideas, which is always a help when learning a new piece. A keen eye and ear for detail are needed to manage accidentals which recur in a bar (e.g the right-hand F♯ in bar 9), and *8ve* signs require care, such as in bars 1 and 32 where the left hand remains at pitch. Initial legato practice may help to establish the all-important fingering for bars 9–10, and bar 11 will benefit from close attention to any co-ordination difficulties.

Rhythm is a vital ingredient for success, and the suggested metronome mark should allow sufficient time to manage the detail. Avoid altering the speed when there are changes of pattern – the ostinato-type figures need particular control – and be aware of the few changes of time signature on the final page. The large range of the keyboard used in bars 4, 15 and 32–6 requires flexible movement of the body in order to anticipate the leaps, which may need memorizing.

Rotation of the hand and forearm will facilitate the right-hand broken octaves at bars 5–8, and these should be sufficiently light to allow the folk-like left-hand melody to project. Either a finger or wrist staccato can be used for the semiquavers in bar 9; in the following bar the contrast of touches must be audible. Accents always add character, especially at unexpected places, and should be differentiated from the gentler tenuto lines used to promote certain notes within the texture.

The clearly marked pedalling is often used to create a 'wash' of sound, contrasting with the clarity of the unpedalled sections. Careful listening will ensure that all changes are clear; the pedal should be lifted for the rests in bars 3 and 35.

Reading the score away from the piano will help in absorbing the music's phrasing and dynamic detail. Your pupil will enjoy exploring the wide tonal range that the piece offers, and should highlight the climax points by controlling the quieter sections. Elements of surprise should be enjoyed, especially the rhythmically free *con fantasia,* at bar 4, and the ending – which is most effective if kept strictly in time.

C:2 Brian Bonsor *Willie Wagglestick's Walkabout*

It is important to choose music that is enjoyable to play, especially for the upper grades when considerable time is invested in exam preparation. This piece, with its amusing title and infectious musical character, is likely to be a sure winner with many candidates.

Facility around the keyboard and an excellent sense of rhythm are essential ingredients for an effective performance, but ultimately the most important factor is a sense of fun! A steady pulse must be maintained throughout, so occasional checking with the metronome will help to highlight any fluctuations which might occur between sections. Although there are four main beats per bar, thinking in two dotted-minim beats should give forward momentum while guarding against too many obtrusive accents.

The two-against-three cross-rhythm in bars 21–3 will need careful practice to ensure the triplets are evenly spaced, with the left hand's notes slotted exactly between the second and third of each group.

Rotating the hand from side to side will facilitate playing the tremolos, which sound best when pedalled and which should be treated as shapely musical effects. A sense of pulse must remain at these points, but a measured number of demisemiquavers is not needed. Although occasional 'dabs' of pedal can highlight the harmonies (e.g. the chords in bar 7), clarity in the fast-moving figuration is always the priority. Slow practice for confidence and precision might be needed at bars 13–16 and 25–8, where the different figures of each hand might upset both synchronization and rhythm.

The predominant dynamic markings are *forte* and *mezzo-forte*, yet there is scope for considerable variety and shape in the right hand; for instance, in bars 6–8 where the descending melodic line suggests a diminuendo through the three bars. Dropping back in tone at the start of crescendos will increase their impact, and accents and tenuto lines will need precise attack, especially when they occur on unexpected offbeat notes. The left hand's accompanying role (for the most part) means that figuration and chords should be deftly balanced.

Phrasing is marked very precisely. The short slurs (e.g. in bars 3–5) – needing clean articulation and quieter thumb notes – highlight the main melodic interest, and contrast with longer phrases, which can be more expansive. A well-graded ritardando and diminuendo in the final three bars will create an effective, 'cool' ending.

C:3 Villa-Lobos *The Tide Came In*

The guitar seems never far away in many Spanish and South American pieces, and this delightful and unusual piece is no exception.

At the four-bar introduction candidates should not be daunted by a key signature in which every note, including F, is flattened. The pedal will sustain the evocative added 6th chords in bar 1, and is indeed the only way to hold the long chord in bars 2–3, above which the guitar-like semiquaver flourish needs clarity and definition. A crescendo and diminuendo over the four bars will reflect the ascending/descending pitch, while the rhythm can be quite free as if to suggest improvisation.

The 'vocal' line begins at bar 5, with the melody in octaves played with tenderness and plenty of shape. Accents should be warm and expressive as befits the character of this section. The left hand's chords – their notes and duration – need to be learnt carefully, and then prominence given to the accented notes. Playing bar 12a (the first-time bar) followed by the repeat from bar 5 will give balance and proportion to this otherwise short folk-melody, in addition to offering the opportunity for varying the tone, perhaps by giving greater importance to the left hand the second time round. Subdividing into quavers at bar 8 will ensure that the final triplet figure begins after the final quaver.

At bars 13–20 the complexities in the texture will need unravelling. Achieving sustained minims and staccato semiquavers in the right hand requires good co-ordination and clear listening. Initial semiquaver practice without the minims will develop clear finger staccato (especially on repeated notes) – after which the held notes may be added. Care is needed to sound all right-hand three-note chords together, remembering that accents should be on the E♭, not the F. The left hand provides rhythmic interest by imposing a characteristic South American 3+3+2 feel to the semiquavers. Practising the left hand alone while the right hand silently holds down its notes will help to develop freedom of movement, and leaning the body slightly towards the treble side will facilitate playing the crossed-hand 4ths. Pedal may be used to give substance to the tone in this *forte* passage: either short 'dabs' on each chord or longer pedals depressing at the start of each bar and releasing on the fourth quaver.

The dal segno must be played, and the player instructed to play the repeat again. The unusual, somewhat abrupt ending needs firm tone and a very short final chord.

C:4 Bartók *Jack-in-the-Box*

Mikrokosmos, a collection of 153 pieces in six volumes, remains Bartók's most important contribution to piano study. This attractive piece from Volume 5, full of folk-like character and energy, should prove both enjoyable and rewarding to learn.

A firm pulse throughout and sprightly rhythmic figures will help to achieve the *scherzando* dance-like character. Entries following long notes (e.g. in bar 9) must enter exactly on time, and swift right-hand movement will ensure confident hand-crossing to the bass register at bar 26. Leger lines above and below the stave need careful reading, and close attention should be paid to the frequent ties in the left-hand part, particularly in bars 22–7. The final six bars, with their mixture of slurs, ties and dynamic changes, also demand clear control – and the final middle C must be held for exactly two bars.

It may be helpful to think of the right-hand notes in bars 47–8 enharmonically, as a descending B major pattern. Choice of tempo may be dictated by the technical demands of these semiquaver couplets, and slow practice may be necessary to gain sufficient wrist and finger flexibility to articulate the slurs clearly.

The composer was fastidious about marking musical detail, so both a keen eye and ear are needed to fulfil his demands. Good independence and organization of the hands will enable clear articulation of each hand's different phrasing. The characteristic rhythmic figure of the opening needs the emphasis on the first not the final note of the three, except in bar 38 where accents are marked. A small hand may experience difficulty with the left-hand fingering designed to create a perfect legato in bars 28–33; a viable alternative would be to slur the thumb and second-finger notes while playing all lower notes with the fifth finger. The grouping of the left-hand quavers in bar 42 suggests phrasing across the beat in couplets.

Nervous candidates often under-project the dynamic contrasts, but they are vital for full musical interest. Four main dynamic levels are used (*piano, mezzo-piano, mezzo-forte* and *forte*), each of which should be clearly defined. The frequent crescendos and diminuendos need careful grading, but the sudden *forte* at bar 35 must take the listener by surprise. There should be differentiation between accents and tenuto lines, the former being played with greater attack, and the player can make the most of the rhythmic lopsidedness caused by stresses on the second beat of the bar.

C:5 Debussy *The Little Shepherd*

Children's Corner, a set of six pieces dedicated by Debussy to his daughter, is similar to Schumann's *Kinderszenen* in that it depicts childhood from an adult's perspective. In *The Little Shepherd* the image evoked is of a shepherd boy playing his reed pipe on a lonely hillside, or perhaps it is that of a fine porcelain figurine in a child's nursery.

The notes are relatively straightforward, with only a few potential trouble-spots at bars 19 and 21–6. The recurrence of an accidental in a bar may well be overlooked, especially E# in bar 19, and the ties in bars 24–6 should be checked carefully. Anchoring on the common A# in both perfect 5ths in bar 24 will help the left hand to move reliably – and the chord at the end of this bar may be better understood enharmonically as E flat major.

To master the complex rhythmic detail, think in crotchet (not quaver) beats, subdivided if necessary, taking care not to rush long notes. Quaver triplets at bars 8, 22–3 and 28 need careful spacing, and the two-against-three rhythm in bar 23 may be simplified for practice by removing the right-hand tie.

The tempo indications can appear puzzling at first sight; yet the composer is specific about diversions from the basic speed of the opening four bars – indicating a return to that tempo at *au Mouvement*. Whether the *Cédez* at bar 9 lasts until the return to tempo at bar 12 is less clear, however. Whatever your decision here, a spirit of rhythmic freedom and spontaneity must be conveyed.

The texture is dependent on well-planned pedal-work. This could be a mixture of legato pedalling to join all chords (e.g. bars 8–9) and direct pedalling, lifting on, for example, the second note of the slurs in bar 5. Holding the pedal from bar 10 to the middle of bar 11 (and similar places) will sustain the widely spaced chord; note, however, that the final chord of the piece lasts for two complete bars.

The sound of a shepherd's pipe, clear and sweet, can be evoked at the start, with a gentle crescendo towards the sustained G# in bar 2. Dynamics are carefully marked throughout – especially the levels of *piano, più piano, pianissimo* and *pianississimo*, each of which must be graded carefully – and frequent diminuendos ensure graceful shaping to the ends of phrases. The main climax at bar 24 is enhanced by an increase in speed; following this, for the final phrase, the *una corda* pedal may be used to create an effect of distance.

C:6 Bill Evans *Time Remembered*

Keen jazzers will put their hearts into this lovely transcription of a favourite standard, with its rich harmonies and free-flowing keyboard style. This may be the nearest some pupils get to creating their own jazz, but equally many might be inspired by this to develop their own improvisation skills.

The piece falls broadly into two main sections of roughly equal length; the first has a full texture divided between the hands, and the second, beginning at bar 15, develops the melody rhythmically over more stable chords.

Although the piece ultimately needs a spacious improvisatory approach to the rhythm, learning strictly in time, perhaps writing in the main beats on the score, will sort out the complexities that appear throughout. The second half may appear daunting rhythmically, but practising the left hand alone will provide a secure framework over which the right hand can place its melodic detail. Clapping exercises switching among quavers, triplets and semiquavers while maintaining a steady beat will help to develop rhythmic fluency.

A large hand, although not essential, will facilitate playing the chords. The left-hand 10ths, which will be beyond the reach of many candidates, can be spread upwards; the grace notes in bars 25–6, however, indicate a downward spread. Care should be taken to read accidentals correctly (bar 6 left hand begins with B♭, not A♭) – and to repeat an accidental in a bar when it recurs.

The choice of tempo is left deliberately free – the pupil can go with whatever will allow the song to breathe yet have a crotchet-beat flow. As a rough guide, however, crotchet = 50 should achieve this. The considerable rhythmic freedom highlights the quasi-improvised character, and should follow the natural shape of each main phrase, which is usually four bars in length.

Dynamics are likewise left to the performer, allowing scope for considerable self-expression. A keen ear together with a flexible wrist and firm fingers will enable the 'sung' melodic lines to be projected clearly above the chordal texture. This style affords plenty of dynamic inflexion, which is often dictated by the shape of the melodic contours. Deciding where the main climaxes occur will see the overall shape of each 'verse' emerge.

A full tonal palette will be achieved by subtle use of quieter levels. Candidates should consider varying the character for the lighter-textured second 'verse', perhaps by playing more wistfully, and the ending can fade away to nothing.